Fact-Finding for Mag

Fourmat Publishing

Fact-Finding for Magistrates

by Sheriff Marcus Stone
and
Judge Ian McLean

London
Fourmat Publishing
1990

ISBN 1 85190 099 3

First published 1990

© 1990 Marcus Stone and Ian McLean
Published by Fourmat Publishing 133 Upper Street
London N1 1QP
Typeset by Action Typesetting Ltd, Gloucester
Printed in Great Britain

Preface

Lay magistrates cope with the overwhelming mass of crimes. Our system of criminal justice is based, primarily, on summary trials in the magistrates' courts. Magistrates have a role in the initiation of trials on indictment and in appeals to the Crown Court. Lay jurors decide the relatively small number of trials on indictment.

Lay justice dominates because fact-finding, recognized as the essence of nearly all trials, depends on the assessment of evidence, not on law. This is so even in a legal framework of rules of evidence and procedure for conducting trials, requirements for proof of guilt, and applying criminal law to the proved facts.

In practice, few cases turn on legal decisions such as the admissibility of crucial evidence, or a no case submission. The real question is almost always one of fact.

With the clerk's advice on law, if required, magistrates decide the facts and reach their findings. Magistrates are chosen for their personal qualities, but this responsibility is based on trust in the judgment of the lay citizen.

Fact-finding depends on practical judgment; evidence is evaluated in the light of common sense and experience of life.

The abilities involved in this task are always capable of improvement. They can be developed by training, by personal court experience, and by absorbing the results of the study and analysis of collective court experience – the basis of this book.

Every case is unique, of course; no amount of experience can justify prejudgment of evidence.

As an example, "I've heard that story before" should never be a ground for rejecting it. Yet familiarity with similar stories may help to identify common flaws in such accounts.

The right kind of guidance can help in fact-finding. But works on criminal law, evidence and procedure have other aims and avoid this key process in criminal trials.

The need for a comprehensive, yet condensed, text on fact-finding, designed for magistrates, is obvious. It is confirmed by the encouraging response to the authors' lectures in official training courses.

This book is intended to meet that need.

By avoiding a "do this" or "do that" approach, the book respects a magistrate's status as a judge of fact. Once the material is assimilated, its use in judgment depends on the trial.

The court experience of even busy magistrates is intermittent and limited. To amplify that experience is the aim of this book.

What is provided is such insight into the essential fact-finding processes of criminal trials as the authors have gained at the bar and on the bench in their combined experience with many thousands of witnesses, for over sixty years. This includes extensive experience of sitting alone in summary trials.

But this is in no way a personal or anecdotal account. The material is presented as an objective analysis for general application where appropriate. It is believed that this insight can hardly fail to help magistrates to develop their skills in fact-finding.

Chapter 1 sets out the legal context of a criminal trial, as essential background.

Chapter 2 shows how the real question of fact emerges, that is, whether the crime was committed or whether the accused was the offender.

To separate truth from persuasion needs familiarity with advocacy. Chapters 3, 4 and 5 explain the advocate's role and techniques.

Chapters 6, 7 and 8 give a full and original analysis of how mistakes and lies are detected — the key to fact-finding.

Chapter 9, on opinion evidence and Chapter 10, on circumstantial evidence, show how facts may be inferred from other perceived facts.

Chapter 11 is a survey of problems with witnesses which often arise in practice.

Chapter 12 sums up salient features of the text as they arise in reaching the verdict.

For full insight into fact-finding, the book is designed to be read as a whole by magistrates of all levels of experience. It could then be used for reference.

The book is also a key to practice for justices' clerks, prosecutors, solicitors, counsel, police and social workers.

The book does not assume any legal knowledge, and may interest journalists and others.

Marcus Stone
Ian G McLean

April 1990

Acknowledgements

For his very constructive and valuable comments on the manuscript, we are grateful to Kerry Barker, LL.B, Barrister, Clerk to the South East Hampshire Justices and Joint Magistrates, Training Officer for Hampshire, although we alone are responsible for anything which merits criticism.

We wish to thank the publishers for their instant appreciation of the concept of this book and their patience, efficiency and cordial co-operation in bringing it to publication. It has been a pleasure to work with them.

Contents

Chapter 1

The legal foundations

Deciding the facts is the key to almost every criminal trial. Although this judgment depends on common sense, it is made in a legal context which must be understood.

Magistrates, as lay judges, are not expected to be lawyers, but they must apply the law. From training and experience they become familiar with basic rules which govern all or most criminal trials. When these are grasped, and reinforced by practice, they become a natural part of a magistrate's judgment. In case of doubt, or when less common points of law arise, the court clerk should be consulted. Although he has no responsibility for fact-finding, it is his duty to ensure that all decisions by magistrates comply with the law.

To state the law, which magistrates should know, is not the aim of this chapter; the following references are intended only to clarify the fact-finding process by focusing on aspects of the law which are related to it.

The relevant topics are criminal procedure; the rules about excluding evidence; the requirements for proof; and criminal law.

1. Criminal procedure

In the courts of the United Kingdom, leading concepts are the adversarial principle; fairness to the accused; and the integrity of advocates. These are expressed in rules of criminal procedure which govern not only trials, but also pre-trial processes such as identification parades, or how

1

confessions are obtained. In this book, the focus is on fact-finding in the criminal trial, although ancillary procedures may be related to that.

A criminal trial is a contest between the prosecution and the defence, which magistrates decide. Traditionally this is seen as a better way to arrive at the truth than a court-directed enquiry. Each party presents a case from a partial point of view, being free to choose what evidence to present. Each can test and challenge the evidence of the other. The court does not initiate any enquiry. It is confined to judging the evidence presented. There are many rules to prevent unfairness. The accused must receive a written statement of the charge, with enough time to prepare a defence, and he may be professionally represented. Oral evidence is led in his presence in open court, not secretly or privately.

An advocate is not expected to believe, test or judge his case. He simply presents it on the information given to him. But in the evidence or in a speech, an advocate must not mislead the court by asserting what he knows to be false or denying what he knows to be true.

The order of trial is laid down by law; it provides for opening and closing speeches, and for the examination-in-chief, cross-examination and re-examination of each witness in turn.

At the close of the prosecution case the bench will consider whether or not there is a case to answer. The defence may submit that there is not, and that the accused should be discharged. If it is decided that there *is* a case to answer, the trial goes on, and the accused is free to give or to lead evidence.

At the close of the case, magistrates retire to consider their findings, which they may reach unanimously or by a majority.

In some disputed points of criminal procedure, questions of fact and law may be mixed. As an example, if there is an issue about whether an identification parade was conducted irregularly, what actually happened is a question of fact, and whether that was irregular is a matter of law.

2. Rules excluding evidence

Facts are proved by evidence, that is, information conveyed by witnesses' testimony, documents or exhibits. Additionally, some facts may be presumed by law or may be proved by judicial notice of well-known matters − of history or nature, for instance. Agreed facts, provided that they are formally admitted, need no proof.

Evidence must be relevant, that is, it must tend to prove or disprove a fact in issue. All relevant evidence is admissible in court unless excluded by law. Evidence is excluded by law because, for example, it is of minimal value; it may refer to facts remote from the issue; or it may be unreliable. The law of evidence is often highly complex. The rules are designed to keep what is put before the court within reasonable bounds.

Most evidence is oral, and is given on oath or affirmation.

The need to decide the admissibility of evidence normally arises when one party objects to evidence elicited by another, or where the court thinks that it is proper to intervene.

Issues of admissibility often arise suddenly and without warning. If the question is material, an adjournment might be offered so that advocates may have time to consider and present their arguments properly. Magistrates may consult the court clerk.

Magistrates should be familiar with aspects of the law of evidence which arise regularly. They must ensure that the trial is fair, and that evidence is admitted or excluded only when this is proper.

(a) Leading questions

As a general rule, in examination-in-chief, an advocate may not ask his own witness leading questions about contested facts. Leading questions are those which suggest the desired answer; for example, "Did he threaten you with a poker?". Acceptable questions are those which follow naturally from previous answers and do not suggest anything new to the witness, for instance, "What did he do then?"; "Was he holding anything?"; "What was it?"; "What did he do with it?"; or "Did he say anything at that time?".

One form of leading question – really a double question – assumes another not yet put to the witness, as in "Where were you standing when he kicked you?", without a previous question about kicking.

The impact of evidence elicited by leading questions is reduced since the advocate, not the witness, may be giving the evidence. If a leading question about a disputed fact is not objected to before it is fully stated, it may suggest the answer to the witness, even if the question is disallowed. Advocates sometimes refrain from objecting to leading questions because they hope for similar latitude, or for some other tactical reason, or because they can foresee the evidence anyway. Evidence given in answer to leading questions put to one's own witness is not inadmissible, but its weight may be reduced.

But it is permissible, and, indeed, efficient, to ask one's witness leading questions about uncontested or explanatory facts, such as the witness's personal details and how she came to be in a position to see the incident in issue, what the witness did, and so on. The more rapidly an advocate can go through surrounding matters, the sooner he can get to the real point.

An advocate can ask his own witness leading questions if, exceptionally, the court grants leave to treat the witness as hostile. The meaning of "hostile" in this context is explained in Chapter 4.

In cross-examination, leading questions are not only allowed – they are typical when evidence is under challenge. But in re-examination, an advocate is subject to the same general rule against asking his own witness leading questions.

There is usually some obvious ground for objections to leading; if so, the objection is often conceded, and the solution is to allow the advocate to reformulate his question.

(b) *The rule against hearsay*

Magistrates should be familiar with the important rule against hearsay. A statement made out of court by a person not called as a witness is inadmissible to prove any fact to which it refers. For instance, if a witness said "A policeman told me that it was a lady driver who had knocked down the cyclist", this evidence is excluded because it is unreliable. The witness may have misheard or misinterpreted what the policeman actually said. The policeman may have been mistaken, biased or untruthful. He is not in the witness box and his evidence cannot be tested by cross-examination.

Hearsay is prohibited in examination-in-chief, cross-examination and re-examination, but there are many exceptions to the rule.

Only a few common exceptions are mentioned here. Such brief references may be misleading. They are no substitute for consulting the court clerk or full study of the rules. If such issues of admissibility arise, advocates and the bench, with the clerk's advice, may have to go into the matter in depth.

Evidence of out-of-court statements may be admissible for some relevant reason other than proving their truth, for example, showing that a statement was in fact made, regardless of its accuracy, may indicate the state of mind of a person who heard it.

Perhaps the most common exception to the rule excluding hearsay arises in relation to "confessions" made by the accused to the police or to some other person in authority. This exception applies to *any* self-incriminating statement or admission adverse to the accused, even if it falls short of a full confession. By statute, relevant evidence of such a confession or statement is admissible, unless certain representations are made.

If the defence claims that a confession was or may have been obtained by oppression, or as a result of anything likely to render it unreliable, the court must exclude evidence of the confession unless the prosecution proves the contrary beyond reasonable doubt. Even without any defence objection, the court may itself require such proof, and even then retains a discretion to exclude evidence of confessions in some circumstances. The law on the admissibility of confessions is complex and it is beyond the scope of this book to deal with it in any detail.

(c) Evidence of character

A recurrent problem concerns evidence of character. The character of prosecution or defence witnesses may be attacked in cross-examination, for example, by referring to their previous convictions. This will be allowed only where it is relevant or has a material bearing on the witness's credit, but not if it is merely vexatious or prejudicial.

In the interests of fairness, cross-examination of the accused as to bad character is excluded by statute but this is subject to many exceptions, often of a complex nature, under which the accused may lose the shield which protects him against such attacks.

The exceptions include situations where evidence of another offence is needed to prove the one charged; where the defence asserts the accused's good character; where the defence makes serious imputations against prosecution witnesses; or where an accused gives evidence against a co-accused.

(d) Miscellaneous

Another exclusionary rule based on fairness to the accused excludes evidence of similar facts.

As a general rule, evidence aimed at showing an accused's misconduct on other occasions, that is, apart from the offence charged, or that he has a disposition to commit an offence of the type charged, is inadmissible. But there is an exception where similar fact evidence is relevant and has a probative value which is greater than its prejudicial effect. In the interests of a fair trial, magistrates have a discretion in this matter.

A general rule of evidence is that witnesses can only speak of facts, and should not state opinions. But qualifications and exceptions to this important rule will be discussed later.

Magistrates may sometimes have to decide whether a particular person can lawfully give evidence, that is, whether the person is a competent witness, and, if so, whether the witness is compellable. The general rule is that anyone is competent and compellable as a witness. Exceptions relate to persons of unsound mind, children, and in some situations, accused and spouse.

A compellable witness who refuses to testify may be subject to penalties, including imprisonment.

Oral evidence is inadmissible unless the witness has taken the oath or made an affirmation in the approved form, with an exception in the case of a young child. In law, no distinction is made between these undertakings.

3. Requirements for proof

To establish guilt, even admissible evidence must meet certain requirements, sometimes about a need for corroboration or warnings, and always about the burden and standard of proof.

As a general rule of law, one witness's evidence is sufficient to prove any fact in issue, for example, the testimony of one eyewitness that the accused committed the crime is enough for conviction.

But it is accepted that there is less risk of wrongly convicting an innocent person if the evidence of one incriminating witness is confirmed by that of another. The term applied to such confirming evidence is "corroboration". It means evidence from an independent source, which tends to confirm, in a material particular, that the offence was committed and committed by the accused.

Although there is no general requirement that evidence must be corroborated, or that the court be warned of the danger of acting on uncorroborated evidence, several exceptions to this arise from law or settled practice in relation to evidence which is considered to be inherently unreliable, such as the evidence of accomplices and of complainants in sexual cases.

Where magistrates are minded to convict on uncorroborated evidence in such a case, they are required to direct themselves about the dangers involved, but having done so, if they are nevertheless convinced by the witness, they may still convict.

Many kinds of evidence can amount to corroboration. Classification would not help.

In a criminal trial the accused is presumed to be innocent unless and until he is proved guilty. The prosecution has the burden of establishing guilt by proving all the essential elements of the crime and that it was the accused who committed it.

The standard of proof which the prosecution must satisfy is to establish the accused's guilt beyond reasonable doubt. Unless that standard is attained, the accused must be acquitted.

The defence need not lead any evidence or prove anything. No comment should be made on an accused's failure to testify.

Where a defence, such as self-defence, is put forward, it is still for the prosecution to disprove it.

4. Criminal law

Crimes generally consist of forbidden acts committed in a culpable state of mind, but the constituents vary. Sometimes, no act is necessary; an omission or the occurrence of an event may be enough. Sometimes an act alone is sufficient without any required state of mind.

But if a mental element is required, it need only be that specified for the particular offence, for example, intention, knowledge or recklessness. A particular consequence may or may not be necessary.

The prosecution must prove *all* the necessary elements for the particular crime charged. Whether or not the prosecution has done so is a mixed question of fact and law. First, magistrates will decide the facts. Then the question will arise whether these facts satisfy the requirements of the criminal law for the crime charged. If necessary, this is a matter on which the justices' clerk may be consulted.

Chapter 2

The real dispute

An outline has been given of the legal framework in which facts are disputed.

The main facts for decision will be:

- whether the crime was committed; and,
- if so, whether the accused committed it.

These facts may be proved by eyewitness evidence; or inferred indirectly from other facts, that is, proved by circumstantial evidence.

In any trial, each side may assert many facts which the other side will not or cannot deny. Although, by law, the prosecution must prove its whole case for conviction, its burden may be reduced if the defence admits any facts formally. The prosecution can do this also. The court would hold such facts as established.

Facts are not admitted formally as often as they might be. The defence usually prefers to admit nothing. The prosecution must then prove the whole case, including unadmitted facts which are not really disputed.

Generally, facts are not disputed because they are true, or there is plenty of evidence to prove them. So the prosecution can usually prove undisputed facts quite easily.

Magistrates will not know about pre-trial discussions between parties, which may focus the dispute. Some agreement is inevitable, whether or not parties reveal this to each other. Even without formal admission of facts, what is unopposed in the prosecution case will become clear as the trial progresses. A priority for magistrates is to identify this common ground; what remains is the real dispute – what the trial is really about.

1. Alternative defences

By law the prosecutor must prove both:

- the commission of the crime (with any necessary mental element); and
- the accused's identity as the offender.

In practice usually only one of these facts is really in dispute. The defence decides which it is to be.

Few defences consist simply of testing or challenging prosecution evidence, without putting a contrary story, which is often, though not always, supported by defence evidence. As a result it becomes impracticable or impossible to contest both of the main facts in the prosecution case. Instead, one is selected as the real question in dispute.

For the purpose of illustration, it is assumed that a crime is alleged to have occurred at a particular time and place (although some may extend over a period).

If the defence consists of a denial that the crime was committed at all – that the legal constituents of the offence are not established – the accused (or some defence witness) must have been at the scene; otherwise no evidence could be given about what happened. The effect of this is almost certainly to eliminate, wholly or substantially, the issue of his identification, especially if he was the only person involved. This could arise in a charge like careless driving.

Thus, where the defence disputes the crime, it tends to concede the question of identification.

The alternative type of defence is that in which the accused claims that he was not at the place when the crime was committed. Whether or not this is supported by an allegation about where else the accused was at that time (a defence of alibi) makes no difference for the present purpose. The essential point is that the accused denies that he was at the scene of the crime.

The accused cannot then, in his own testimony, dispute the prosecution evidence about what happened at the scene of the alleged crime. Accordingly, identification will become the only real issue of fact.

In these model situations, the alternative selected by the defence becomes the real issue. If the defence denies the crime, it does not contest identity; if it denies identity, it does not contest the crime. While this is not an absolute rule, it will be found to apply in almost every trial.

2. Classification of crimes

For practical purposes, crimes may be classified into result-crimes; conduct-crimes; and object-crimes. A *result-crime* is one which is committed only if it includes a specific result; thus death is an essential element of murder. A *conduct-crime* consists of a forbidden act, but needs no result, as in indecent exposure. An *object-crime* involves a forbidden connection with some object, for example, possession of an offensive weapon in a public place.

The typical features of each group of crimes has a bearing on whether the real dispute is likely to be about the commission of the crime, or about identity. The key to this is the distinction between tangible and durable facts on the one hand, and intangible and transient facts on the other.

Tangible facts can be perceived by the senses, and may be durable, for example, the fact that a window is broken. These facts are usually easy to prove, and are therefore unlikely to be disputed. They differ from intangible facts, such as mental states; and transient facts, such as observable but rapid incidents, which leave no physical traces. These are hard to prove and are often disputed.

This difference in the ease of proof is a key to whether the real dispute is likely to be about the crime or not.

(a) Result-crimes

Result-crimes are the most serious category, and include crimes of violence causing injury or death; sexual crimes such as rape or buggery; crimes of dishonesty leading to the transfer of property; road traffic crimes causing damage, injury or death; or acts which cause criminal damage to property.

Physical results, such as wounds, death, signs of sexual violation, removal of goods, or damage, are a common feature of these crimes. These results are generally quite specific and are easily attributable to the criminal act.

Also, these results are likely to be permanent, as in the case of a burnt-out police car, or they last long enough for abundant evidence of them to be available, as in the case of stab wounds.

It is not easy to be mistaken about such facts, to invent them if they do not exist, or to deny them falsely if they do exist. Therefore the results of crimes in this class are not generally in dispute. This takes the prosecution a long way towards proving the commission of the crime.

Of course a mental component, eg knowledge or intention, may be an essential element of the crime. But it can usually be inferred from the physical situation, as when a child has been battered. Thus the fact that a crime was committed is unlikely to be disputed, and magistrates can usually expect *identity* to be the real issue in a result-crime.

(b) Conduct-crimes

A conduct-crime needs no physical result. It is committed by some prohibited act in itself intangible or transient. Examples include forms of indecency without physical contact; blackmail; threatening someone with a knife; and disorderly conduct in the street.

Attempts to commit result-crimes fall within this category, since the conduct stops before it produces the result which is necessary for the completed crime.

Since in a conduct-crime there will usually be no physical traces of the crime, it is likely to require proof by eye-witness evidence which will often be in sharp conflict. Such evidence is open to mistake, bias or dishonesty. It often consists of assertion and contradiction. Therefore, the commission of the crime is likely to be the real issue, because of the opportunities for conflict in testimony, and the difficulties of proof. Also, the prevalence of eyewitness evidence for both parties may eliminate identity as an issue.

(c) Object-crimes

Object-crimes consist of some prohibited relationship to an object. Unlike result-crimes, they do not lead to any result, and unlike conduct-crimes, they require more than an act. Examples are "going equipped" by having an article for use in burglary away from one's abode; unauthorised possession of controlled drugs; and possession of an obscene article for publication for gain.

Object-crimes include both tangible and intangible elements. Usually, the tangible facts are the objects – the tools, the drugs, the obscene article – which are usually produced in evidence. The intangible facts may be questions about the nature of the object, but more often they concern the offender's relationship to the object and the surrounding circumstances. For example, whether or not the accused was aware that the video recorder he bought was stolen; or whether or not he had possession of controlled drugs found in the boot of a borrowed motor car. Here, evidence about the intangible facts – whether about the object or the accused's relationship to it – may be vulnerable to challenge as mistaken or untruthful.

There are too many types of object-crimes to make possible any sound prediction about whether the crime or identity is more likely to be the real question in such offences, but it would be exceptional for both to be in issue.

3. Identity as the real dispute

The identity of the accused as the offender may be proved by any of the following kinds of evidence, either alone or in combination: eyewitness evidence of recognition, resemblance or a distinctive characteristic; circumstantial evidence; or evidence of a full confession or partial admission.

To destroy alibi evidence, is not, by itself, and without some positive evidence implicating the accused, proof of the accused's identity as the offender; for example, a false alibi may be an attempt to boost a weak but genuine defence.

Visual recognition of the accused by eyewitnesses as the person who committed the crime, if accepted as accurate beyond any reasonable doubt, proves his identity as the offender.

Visual evidence of resemblance or that the accused and the offender have some distinctive characteristics, are merely items of circumstantial evidence.

Circumstantial evidence will be dealt with in a later chapter. Here, it will suffice to say that if witnesses speak of separate facts which, in combination, lead magistrates to infer beyond reasonable doubt that the accused was the offender, identity has been proved.

Physical or scientific evidence may often be very important in linking the accused with the crime.

If evidence is given, usually by police, that the accused made a full confession of guilt, and magistrates find, beyond reasonable doubt, that the confession was made and that it was truthful, the accused is proved to be the offender.

Evidence of a partial admission may be an item of circumstantial evidence.

As has been demonstrated, a defence based on a positive version of the facts must adopt one of two alternatives: either that the accused was at the scene of the crime, or that he was not.

Where the accused admits that he was present, the real dispute will be about what he was doing — relating his admitted presence to the alleged criminal acts.

In respect of the evidence, the court will be concerned with the accuracy of observation of the accused's conduct, in decisions about identification. Mistakes of observation and of memory can occur in such circumstances — especially in a fast-moving and confusing situation involving a number of people. The possibility of lying by motivated witnesses on either side must also be taken into account.

Where the accused denies being at the scene of the crime, he need neither say nor prove where he was at the time, but he will often specify an alibi, or claim that in view of the lapse of time, he has forgotten where he was, but it was not at the scene of the crime.

Where the defence denies the accused's presence at the scene of the crime, it will attack any contrary evidence. Eyewitness evidence of visual identification will be challenged.

If the accused is implicated by circumstantial evidence, it may be difficult to challenge the facts from which guilt is inferred, especially if supported by several independent and unconnected witnesses, who seem to be sincere. But the defence may still argue that guilt should not be inferred — or at least, not beyond reasonable doubt.

An accused should know if he was there, and would only rarely be mistaken, for example, if he was in a drunken coma. So he is usually cross-examined on the basis that he is lying about his whereabouts. It may be unlikely for alibi witnesses associated with the accused to be mistaken about his identity or about the time and place. So they too, are usually accused of lying.

Alibi witnesses may describe a real event when the accused was truly with them, but lie about when that was. They may have staged such an incident so that genuine, and therefore persuasive, evidence may support a lie about the date or time.

But the prosecution may contend that alibi witnesses are mistaken about having seen the accused, if he was not well-known to them, or if there were poor conditions of observation.

Chapter 3

The role of the advocate

1. The adversarial system

In our adversarial system of criminal justice, magistrates decide the outcome of a contest between the prosecution and the defence, but do not direct the enquiry. Advocates present their cases as they see fit, choosing what evidence to lead, to accept, or to dispute. The objective of advocacy is to persuade the court to accept a particular version of the facts.

A prosecutor *must* lead evidence to support his case. A defence advocate may or may not do so. A prosecutor or defence advocate need not test, believe, or judge his own case. These are questions for the court. But he should test and, where proper, challenge, his opponent's evidence, irrespective of his personal opinion about it, provided that he bases this on his instructions and the information given to him.

A good advocate presents his case as a comprehensible and persuasive story. By his handling of evidence, he will highlight the real issues of fact, and explain how the law applies to any aspect of the case. His contentions will be explicit and clear. But partiality and tactics will pervade an advocate's conduct of the case. This is expected and in evaluating the evidence, magistrates should be fully aware of the underlying thrust to win.

Evidence is obtained in three ways. In examination-in-chief, an advocate questions witnesses whom he calls. Their evidence should be relevant to the issue and sufficient in law for its purpose. In cross-examination, an advocate questions witnesses called by another party, either constructively to secure evidence helpful to his case, or destructively to show that their evidence is unacceptable for one reason or another. In re-examination an advocate questions his own witness again, on matters arising out of cross-examination, and tries to undo any harmful effect which it may have caused.

2. Professional standards

In considering the tactics of advocacy the ethical limits on an advocate's freedom need to be taken into account. Professional ethics require that, despite his contentious role in the adversarial conflict, an advocate should conduct himself in court with personal integrity rather than by trying to win at all costs. Improper conduct in court may expose him to criticism, reprimand or worse, and evidence obtained by objectionable means, might be excluded. Nor should an advocate become emotionally involved; professional detachment is always expected.

A prosecutor's duty is to present the evidence fairly, with the aim of helping the court to reach a proper verdict — not to secure a conviction. Thus, he should elicit in court, or disclose to the defence, any material evidence in his possession, even if it favours the accused.

A prosecutor's cross-examination of defence witnesses — especially an accused — ought to be fair and have a sound basis. A prosecutor should concede facts which he accepts, although they help the defence. He may attack the accused's character if he is entitled to do so. But it is proper to do this only where it is relevant and not simply prejudicial. The defence has no corresponding obligation to disclose any evidence helpful to the prosecution. Its duty is best seen in the light of any advocate's duty to the court. It is a basic duty that an advocate must not knowingly mislead or deceive the court. The magistrates' finding will show that at least one side has presented a mistaken or untruthful version of the facts, but the advocate is not to be held responsible if he conducted the case in good faith on the basis of his instructions and the information given to him.

Thus, a defence advocate may assert facts based on his instructions only. He must not attack evidence which he knows to be true, although he may test it for accuracy. He must not ask questions merely to insult or annoy.

An advocate to whom the accused confesses his guilt is not obliged to inform the court of that, but his duty not to mislead or deceive the court arises acutely. In this, albeit rare, situation, he must not assert or deny any facts which contradict the accused's guilt. He can only conduct a "legal" defence, for example, by objecting to the court's jurisdiction; the legal basis of the charge; the admissibility of evidence; or he may argue that in law there is no case to answer.

Although his advocate will advise the accused, it is for the accused himself to decide whether to plead guilty or not guilty (and in the trial, whether or not to give evidence). Whatever his beliefs or suspicions, it is the advocate's duty to defend the accused, subject to compliance with the obligations explained above.

The principle is that every accused person, irrespective of his character, the nature of the crime charged, and, even, in the situation previously described, his guilt, is entitled to be represented professionally. The advocate is expected to do and say everything for the accused which he would do for himself if he had the professional skill. This creates a fair balance between the professional ability of the prosecutor, and the general lack of it in most citizens. But of course, any accused has the right to represent himself.

Like any tribunal, magistrates are entitled to rely on advocates to fulfil their duty to the court, by not misleading or deceiving them, knowingly, about the facts.

As lay justices, they are also entitled to expect that advocates will take care not to mis-state the law, although they may offer arguments or interpret it in favour of their own case. If an advocate does mis-state the law, his opponent's arguments and the advice of the court clerk act as built-in checks.

In disputes of fact, an advocate's professional qualification gives him no special status or authority. Fact-
finding is based on common sense, not law, although
decisions are made within a framework of legal rules.

It is essential that magistrates should distinguish an
advocate's duty to the court, on which they are entitled to
rely, from his contentions in evidence or in argument
about facts. These are partial, and are designed to
persuade the court to reach the finding which he seeks.
Here it is the advocate's duty to his client which is
dominant. In performing that duty, he may also obscure
the facts. Insight into the tactics of advocacy can help
magistrates to see through a smokescreen of persuasion
to the truth.

An overview of the advocate's general role has been
given. Some salient features of the tactics will now be
reviewed. Speeches are covered in this chapter, and the
examination and cross-examination of witnesses in the
next two chapters.

3. Speeches

(a) The prosecution

Summary criminal procedure allows each party one, and
sometimes two, speeches. The basic pattern is a
prosecution opening speech and a defence closing speech.

In simple cases, prosecutors often omit opening speeches;
in others they may give a brief outline of the main facts to
be proved, and how they will prove them. Here, clarity
rather than persuasion would be the aim.

If the facts are complex or there are many witnesses, the
prosecutor's opening speech may have tactical
importance. While explaining the case clearly, it may also
start the persuasive process. Magistrates must take care
not to treat a prosecutor's optimistic opening statements
as some kind of evidence, or worse, as proved facts.

If a prosecutor has evidence to support the facts which he states, to exaggerate its value in an opening speech may be counter-productive. Evidence may not prove facts inevitably. Proof depends on the court's judgment; it is discourteous and imprudent to seem to predict or dictate the court's mental processes.

As the first version of the disputed facts, a prosecutor's opening speech may have a tactical advantage, by organizing what may become a mass of details, imparting a structure to the trial, focusing on the real point, and integrating facts into a coherent and easily remembered story. It is, though, only an introduction.

(b) The defence

The defence closing speech may also have tactical importance. The whole case may be summed up in a way favourable to the accused, at the final stage before magistrates retire to reach their finding.

A good speech will present the defence as a coherent and credible human story, not a list of points on a scorecard. All the main facts and essential evidence will be stated in one total view which is clear, convincing and easy to recall. Visual imagery often helps. It will focus parties' contentions on the real issue (the crime or identity), stressing what counts, meeting criticisms or doubts, and highlighting the agreements or conflicts in evidence.

This may be an excellent opportunity to complete the cross-examination. For example, if the defence advocate withheld a final question, to avoid an unwanted answer or alerting his opponent, he can now, without these risks, ask the court to infer the desired conclusion.

Again, seemingly minor facts from various sources may be built into something significant.

Perhaps the most common tactic in defence closing speeches is to list inconsistencies in prosecution evidence. This may be weak if it only exaggerates the importance of normal errors of observation and memory about details, and strong if it exploits material contradictions.

To criticize the accuracy of observation or memory of eye-witnesses seldom succeeds by itself. Often, the key is whether or not to trust the witness who assesses the reliability of his own evidence. A defence closing speech may therefore focus on flaws like bias or irresponsibility in prosecution witnesses, and on the soundness of defence witnesses.

Where visual identification is an issue, a defence speech may stress the necessity of distinguishing evidence of resemblance from evidence of recognition.

Other final defence arguments may refer to the effects on prosecution evidence of delay, discussion between witnesses, or pre-trial police procedure.

The defence closing speech may mount an attack on prosecution witnesses as untruthful by referring to their character, motives and the inconsistency or improbability of their evidence.

A witness who must be in no doubt about the facts, and whose evidence is said to be seriously inaccurate, can only be lying; yet a common defence submission is that some such witnesses, often police officers, are mistaken. Magistrates may see this as an insincere, half-hearted and weak challenge.

It is at this stage that incriminating circumstantial evidence – the underlying facts or the inference from them – may be opposed. The facts are often beyond dispute. Generally, it is the adverse inference to be drawn from them which is criticized in the defence speech, by suggesting other inferences which are consistent with innocence, and emphasizing that guilt must be proved beyond any reasonable doubt. Circumstantial evidence is often open to such objections, as it involves probability.

The defence advocate may also argue that the evidence of the accused and defence witnesses, which directly contradicts adverse inferences from circumstantial evidence, should be accepted.

In any speeches by any party, magistrates are more likely to be impressed if adverse points which are obvious, are confronted and conceded, instead of being ignored in the hope that the bench will fail to see them.

Whether or not closing speeches refer to the burden and standard of proof, the need for corroboration, warnings, or care in regard to some kinds of evidence, magistrates, aided by the court clerk, are deemed to be aware of these requirements, and must apply them whether or not they are reminded about them in any case.

Magistrates ought to know what advocates are trying to do when they elicit evidence. Their aim is always tactical — to bring out the evidence in a way which will influence its assessment and the court's finding in the desired direction.

Chapter 4

Examination-in-chief and re-examination

In examination-in-chief an advocate questions his own witness. Usually he obtains evidence which he expects to support his case. But sometimes a witness does not come up to expectations, and in extreme cases he can be treated as hostile – that is, more or less like a witness for the opponent's side.

1. Prosecution evidence

The examination-in-chief of prosecution witnesses must establish all the elements needed for conviction, that is, (1) that the crime was committed; and (2) that it was the accused who committed it.

We have seen that, usually, only one of these main facts is in dispute, but the prosecutor must still prove the other undisputed fact – which should cause no difficulty.

All the main facts in the prosecution case must be proved by evidence which is admissible, relevant, sufficient in law, and of enough weight to prove them beyond any reasonable doubt.

Eyewitness evidence of the crime and the offender's identity is common, but identity is often established by circumstantial evidence.

2. Defence evidence

As the defence need not prove anything, sometimes it does

not call any witnesses, but conducts a "legal" defence without asserting any facts.

In practice, however, more often than not the defence presents evidence of an alternative version of the facts. Even if that version is not established, it may at least create a reasonable doubt about the prosecution version.

3. Clarity and persuasion

If evidence obtained in examination-in-chief is unclear, it may either not be understood, or it may be understood in a harmful way. Also, evidence which is not properly grasped may not be remembered.

If facts are inherently complex or confusing, it is part of the advocate's skill to clarify them. But too often, simple situations are described in a jumbled way which makes them incomprehensible – often because advocates, familiar with the case, make assumptions which are not conveyed to the court.

A court may ask questions to clarify isolated points, but responsibility for presenting the whole case clearly, belongs to the advocate.

In examining a witness, clarity of evidence depends on a number of factors, including quality of speech, language, setting the scene initially in terms of place, time and persons, the sequence of events, repetition, varying the angle, or additional details.

Evidence is expected not only to convey comprehensible information, but also, where it contradicts other evidence, to persuade. In court, persuasion should be a rational process, but in any human tribunal, feelings and intuitions enter into the evaluation process somewhere. This need not conflict with rationality.

Examples of effective persuasion abound in daily life – advertising is an obvious example – but the techniques for doing this are often neglected in presenting evidence in court.

The first element in persuasion is to attract the listener's attention. Without this, the message is lost. Attention is a matter of interest. Interest must be aroused initially and maintained until the end.

Evidence is likely to have a greater impact if it is presented in the form of a human story with a strong visual content, and realistic details of the facts and of the involvement of persons. Parts of the story which are under enquiry at any stage, should be related to the whole story, and the main theme should recur again and again.

4. Leading questions

We have seen in Chapter 1 that, in examination-in-chief, a general rule of evidence prohibits leading questions (those framed in a way which suggests the desired answer), but that the apparent difficulties caused by this rule can usually be overcome.

Leading questions are excluded because they may have the effect that advocates, not witnesses, would be testifying. They invite "yes" or "no" answers; the evidence becomes too partial; witnesses are deprived of their personalities, and seem to be reduced to puppets. Leading questions in this way eliminate material which may help the court in its evaluation of the reliability or credibility of evidence.

However, there are many exceptions to the rule which excludes leading questions. They cannot be defined precisely, but examples should explain them sufficiently.

Essentially, the exceptions include questions about undisputed facts, for example, about secondary matters not linked directly with the real issue. This includes the personal details of the witness, how he came to observe the event, and introductory or explanatory narrative.

Other exceptions are questions in regard to which advocates do not object to leading, for example, about facts accepted as already proved or questions to which the answer is inevitable.

Answers given to leading questions, before objection, are not inadmissible, but their weight may be reduced if magistrates think that the witness was unduly instructed by the form of the question. On the other hand, some facts are so stark that the answer is bound to be the same, whether the question is leading or not, for example, "Inspector, on the night of the 20th of June was that police van destroyed by fire?".

In practice, great use is made of leading questions by common consent. They save time and allow advocates to reach the important topics rapidly and efficiently.

5. Controlled or free evidence

How closely an advocate controls his own witnesses may vary and can affect both the content of, and the impression made by, their evidence.

By tightly framed questions, an advocate may proceed, step by step, without leading, but without allowing the witness to elaborate or diverge. For example, "Who was in the room?"; "Where was X?"; "What did X do?". The aim is to prevent one's own witness from giving evidence which is not wanted, by rambling and straying from the point, or introducing irrelevant, prejudicial or harmful material.

Close control allows an advocate to select evidence which he wants and exclude what he does not want. But while this, in effect, permits him to edit testimony for persuasive purposes, it is subject to ethical limits in view of the advocate's duty not to mislead or deceive the court deliberately.

Expert witnesses could often give more complete evidence, or could qualify the evidence which they give, more fully than the advocate who called them allows.

Where an advocate thinks that his opponent has edited evidence either tactically or improperly, the remedy of cross-examination to expose this is open to him.

Magistrates need to be alert to the possibility that evidence is incomplete or distorted. While they cannot, themselves, explore undisclosed material, they are entitled to take this impression into account in evaluating the evidence which has been given.

By controlling an examination-in-chief strictly, an advocate can ensure that the evidence is presented in an orderly sequence and that nothing important is omitted.

But if control is carried too far, the evidence may omit detail, and elements of the witness's personal involvement, so that it lacks spontaneity and obscures his personality.

Magistrates may then find the evidence less convincing, and harder to assess, because of the lack of helpful material.

Again, a witness, if pressed, may stretch his recollection beyond the point at which he is sure of it, and thus testify inaccurately. If this inaccuracy is later exposed by cross-examination or contradictory evidence, the case which that witness supports may be damaged.

The opposite approach for an advocate is to allow his witness the maximum of freedom by drawing his attention to the event and then permitting him to tell his story in his own way with as little prompting as possible.

Genuine testimony given in this way will be more natural and spontaneous and may thus be more impressive. It will not seem to be the result of coaching. Instead of "yes" or "no" answers, the story may be more vivid and more likely to inspire trust. But on the other hand, if the evidence is false, its insincerity may be more obvious if it is given freely.

These comments, of course, refer to tendencies; there can be no rules about the assessment of either form of testimony.

In practice, advocates are usually cautious and they control their witnesses in examinations-in-chief. They are concerned that something harmful may emerge if they let their witnesses testify freely. The risk depends on the nature of the evidence and on the witness.

The kind of questions asked in examination-in-chief may assist the bench or they may tend to obscure the facts.

It is helpful to magistrates if the advocate puts questions which are brief, clear, simple, and confined to one point at a time.

On the other hand, advocates usually follow the maxim of only asking a question to which they know the answer – and which, of course is expected to be favourable. They will therefore refrain from asking a question which might elicit an adverse answer, but which might be illuminating to magistrates.

However, it is the function of the opponent to draw out such contradictory evidence.

6. Anticipating cross-examination

If the defence gives evidence in a trial, the finding will turn on the conflict of evidence given by two sets of witnesses. In cross-examination the two versions of the facts are brought into direct confrontation. In examining his witnesses a good advocate will locate possible weaknesses in their evidence and will forestall any likely challenge in cross-examination. This can be helpful to the bench.

In the examination-in-chief an advocate who foresees that his evidence will be attacked, must decide whether or not to reveal weaknesses in his case to his opponent and to the court.

Sometimes, without being disclosed, weaknesses can be dealt with by reinforcing certain other aspects of the evidence. On the other hand, disclosing a weakness in the examination-in-chief may have advantages. It may seem frank; the point may be likely to emerge anyway; the difficulty may be coped with more easily in examination-in-chief; its impact may be less then; and it prepares the witness. Drawbacks are that disclosing a weakness may suggest something which an opponent might not have realized: or that to take a possible challenge seriously, may seem to lend it weight.

Magistrates should be quick to see that such pivotal issues arise in the examination-in-chief, expressly or by implication; they may be crucial to the finding. They are often signalled by a change of direction in the line of questioning about an important topic and the use of such phrases as, "If it were to be suggested that ... what would you say?", so that the advocate puts himself in his opponent's place.

An example might be, in examination-in-chief, to ask a prosecution witness who has identified the accused visually, whether he has not mistaken him for another person of similar appearance. Here, the prosecutor anticipates the inevitable defence cross-examination on that point because he knows that another person who resembles the accused was involved. By raising the issue himself, he takes the wind out of his opponent's sails and probes the matter in a way which favours his case and which prepares the witness for the challenge.

Accordingly, in the examination-in-chief of any witness, magistrates should be alert for the emergence of such significant issues.

7. Re-examination

After his witness has been cross-examined, an advocate has the right to re-examine him, to counteract any damage which may have been caused. But the rules of evidence confine re-examination to matters arising from cross-examination, about which the witness may be allowed to amplify or explain his evidence. This is not a chance for further examination-in-chief, for example, by adding to or emphasizing it, or by introducing new material. Problems for the bench may arise in deciding the admissibility of a line of re-examination, if the cross-examination referred to a topic indirectly, but not expressly.

A good advocate will only re-examine his witness at all, or on any topic, where this is necessary. Re-examination is often omitted or is very brief.

If the damage caused by cross-examination was minor, re-examination may emphasize adverse points. If the damage was substantial, re-examination may be ineffective. From an advocate's point of view, it may be preferable to counteract the damage in other ways, such as by leading contradictory evidence or by argument.

As in examination-in-chief, leading questions are prohibited in principle, and certainly on disputed matters. But by this stage it will have become clear that many matters are not in dispute. In referring to them, harmless leading questions can direct a witness's attention efficiently and quickly to the real point for enquiry.

Chapter 5

Cross-examination

Insight into the role of cross-examination can contribute to sound fact-finding. A detailed grasp of the techniques is unnecessary. It is enough to understand the nature, aims and limitations of cross-examination.

Cross-examination is a stage of procedure when an advocate questions another advocate's witness. Its essence is that one point of view confronts another.

In our system of justice, if an advocate's contentions are contrary to the facts, cross-examination, however skilful, is not expected to destroy the truth. Indeed, it often strengthens adverse evidence by testing it without damage. In this way, it serves the cause of justice, although that cross-examiner's case fails. But the advocate is not deemed to know the facts; his duty is to present a case.

1. Aims of cross-examination

Whether or not to cross-examine must be decided in respect of both witnesses and topics. Good advocates cross-examine for sound reasons only. According to the context, cross-examination may be essential, desirable, unnecessary or counter-productive.

Good cross-examination ends as soon as the aim is attained or is seen to be unattainable. It is therefore as brief as possible.

The most common fault is to go over the evidence-in-chief aimlessly, often in pointless detail, hoping for some change or helpful material. This may suggest a weak case, and emphasize adverse evidence by repetition and elaboration, thereby converting rather harmless evidence into a real obstacle.

Cross-examination may be conducted with either constructive or destructive aims, both of which are discussed later in this chapter (see pages 37 to 49).

2. Failure to cross-examine

If a party fails to cross-examine an opponent's witness where it would be proper to do so, he incurs the risk that he may be deemed to have accepted that witness's evidence.

An advocate is expected, in cross-examination, to challenge any part of the evidence which is inaccurate, and to put his own case to the witness so far as the facts are known to him.

Giving the witness a chance to explain creates a proper foundation for the cross-examiner to lead contradictory evidence and to contend that the evidence of the opponent's witness should be rejected.

Failure by the defence advocate to cross-examine prosecution witnesses, by putting the accused's story to them, may give rise to the suggestion that the accused's version of events was invented after hearing the prosecution evidence.

3. Limits of cross-examination

The right to cross-examine is limited by the rules which govern the admissibility of any evidence, with some added provisions. The law of evidence is not the subject of this book, but attention is drawn here to some important areas.

Any witness may be cross-examined. Co-accused may cross-examine each other and their respective witnesses.

A court should be familiar with the restrictions on attacking an accused's character and the statutory exceptions.

Cross-examination is not confined to the issues raised in the examination-in-chief. Subject to the rules of evidence, it may relate to any of the issues in the case, or to the credit of witnesses.

Cross-examination as to credit, and especially attacks on character, should be relevant to the witness's credibility, and should be made on the basis of reasonable information only.

Insulting or vexatious questions, intended only to harass or annoy a witness, should not be allowed. Witnesses are entitled to consideration in a court of law even when their evidence is challenged.

The general rule is that unfavourable evidence given under cross-examination about collateral issues is final; this means that while the court need not accept it as true, the cross-examiner cannot call further evidence to contradict the witness. There are, though, exceptions to this rule which are not examined in this book.

4. Tactics

Effective cross-examination is based on formulating a clear aim, and adopting modes of questioning designed to attain it.

In cross-examination there is no special way of questioning which by itself has a magical, incisive and penetrating effect; the skill consists of adapting questions to the situation, and directing them with a clear purpose.

Leading questions are allowed in cross-examination and are the usual form. Typically, the cross-examiner asserts something with which the witness then agrees or disagrees. But questions should not be put in such a form as to create an argument between the advocate and the witness.

If co-operative witnesses called by the opponent give helpful evidence, it may have more weight if it is elicited without leading, as in examination-in-chief.

Witnesses are usually cross-examined under strict control, to stop them from introducing, repeating or emphasizing unfavourable evidence.

Thus, cross-examiners generally avoid questions to which they cannot reasonably foresee the answers.

Questions must be clear; otherwise a witness may have a line of escape by claiming that he did not understand something.

The rate of questioning may vary for tactical reasons. Rapid questions may be asked to confuse an untruthful witness and give him no time to invent. Slow and deliberate questions may highlight a witness's hesitation, or may commit him irrevocably to some position which will later be demolished.

The sequence of questions may be designed to confuse an untruthful witness, for example, if they are asked in a random sequence, he will be unprepared, and may find it hard to recall what he said previously. A truthful witness may have no difficulty.

A false witness may be thrown off his guard if an important question is concealed in a series of unimportant ones.

To discredit lying witnesses or extract the truth, cross-examiners may mislead them intentionally, in indirect ways, but without deceiving them explicitly. This is only acceptable within limits, and so, for example, evidence or facts must not be misrepresented.

A cross-examiner, having mastered the facts, may ask questions in such a way as to suggest ignorance of them, so as to lead an untruthful witness into a trap through over-confidence.

Questions may suggest that a certain answer is wanted, with the aim of inducing a false witness to give the contrary and wanted answer.

Answers to a series of questions put to different witnesses from different angles may add up to the wanted but omitted conclusion, although none of the witnesses realized this.

The range of tactical options open to cross-examiners is wide, but the main option is between constructive and destructive tactics. The following brief outline of these will complete the background information about cross-examination which magistrates require.

5. Constructive cross-examination

A cross-examiner's constructive aim would be to elicit positive and favourable evidence from another party's witness, with which to support or build his own case.

Another party's witnesses are often honest and non-partisan, and therefore likely to co-operate in the cross-examination. Dishonest or biased witnesses are still constrained by their oath or affirmation, and the factual context, and they may also make concessions, albeit with reluctance. Favourable evidence obtained from another party's witnesses is often regarded as having some weight.

There are four main kinds of constructive tactics:

(a) placing emphasis on favourable evidence;
(b) introducing new and favourable meanings of evidence given in chief;
(c) drawing out new facts which were omitted from the evidence-in-chief; and
(d) introducing an alternative version of the facts stated in the evidence-in-chief.

In *emphasis* the cross-examiner accepts some favourable part of the evidence-in-chief and intensifies its effect, by, for example, drawing attention to it, repeating it, adding details or making it more vivid. It would be unwise to do this if there was a risk that the witness might retract the favourable evidence already given.

A cross-examiner may be able to create *new meanings* for evidence-in-chief. With a friendly and indirect approach the cross-examiner may accept the underlying facts stated by the witness, while gradually insinuating that they mean something other than what he originally said. This would be done by cautious leading questions, and bringing the witness to agree to minor adjustments here and there, which tilt the evidence in the desired direction. It may be necessary to refer to contradictory evidence.

If, finally, the witness accepts the new meaning, or even that it is possible, the cross-examination has had some positive result. But if the witness firmly rejects a reasonable new explanation, his evidence may appear to be untruthful or biased. He may, indeed, be discredited in other parts of his evidence. Such tactics may create reasonable doubt about a fact which the prosecution must prove for guilt, or, at least, weaken an unfavourable meaning so that it is overcome by other evidence.

A cross-examiner can often draw out *new facts* omitted from the examination-in-chief, depending on how complete it was, and the witness's co-operation. New evidence may have more weight if it is obtained without leading questions, but they may be essential with a reluctant witness.

Material facts disclosed for the first time in cross-examination may be impressive. If they were excluded because the opponent edited the evidence by failing to ask appropriate questions, his case may be damaged; if he did ask such questions, the witness who omitted the facts, may seem to be reluctant – although this may strengthen his new evidence.

The harmful effects of failure to put one's case to a witness who knows the facts were discussed as an aspect of failure to cross-examine, generally. The advantages of putting the *alternative case*, as a form of constructive tactics, may now be considered.

Doing this is tactically essential. It defines a party's position and it may have a suggestive effect on the court, even where the witness denies the case, as is common. Some cross-examiners do this with some degree of role-playing, but this, however reasonable, assertive or impressive, is not evidence. The witness's response is evidence, even if it seems false or unconvincing, and is not accepted.

6. Destructive cross-examination

Tactics of cross-examination are mainly destructive. Their aim is to weaken or destroy harmful evidence by challenging it as untruthful or mistaken.

(a) Effect of destructive tactics

Even if cross-examination does not destroy belief in evidence totally, it may succeed by creating doubt, especially in prosecution evidence. Without concluding that a witness is lying or mistaken, magistrates may view his credibility as too doubtful to be trusted, or they may regard his reliability as unacceptable.

Where evidence is not accepted, because of disbelief or doubt, the effect on the outcome of the case will depend on which party's case needed that evidence, and on the prosecution's onus of proof.

Rejected evidence need not prove the contrary unless it follows logically; for example, to expose an accused's false denial that he was the driver, means that he was the driver. But a lie about being in Oxford does not put him in Andover.

It is unrealistic to expect a lying witness to retract what he said, substitute the truth, or to become so inarticulate as to nullify his evidence. His strong original reason for lying is intensified by fear of the consequences of exposure. Cross-examination of a lying witness rarely succeeds at once. It should only be expected to weaken evidence. If the evidence is destroyed, this usually occurs in three stages – weakening it in cross-examination; leading contradictory evidence; and attacking it in the final speech. Exceptionally, of course, the exposure of lying during cross-examination is so overwhelming that the outcome is beyond doubt.

The effects of challenging evidence as mistaken may vary. Honest witnesses sometimes concede doubts or change evidence which is challenged as mistaken, unless bias or vanity impedes this. But again, some honest witnesses may insist firmly on their mistaken evidence, and their sincerity may be persuasive. Again, the decision about that evidence may depend on the same three stages in the trial — weakening the evidence in cross-examination; leading contradictory evidence; and attacking it in the final speech.

It is a typical defence problem whether or not to call the accused and other evidence. The defence may simply cross-examine to put the prosecution to its proof and justify a no case to answer submission, or to raise a reasonable doubt. Prosecution witnesses do not often establish facts favouring the defence, but it may happen; a prosecutor has a duty to call such witnesses.

Even where a right to cross-examine cannot be denied — a veto always being risky — much cross-examination simply wastes court time, or even harms the cross-examiner's case.

Minor points or feeble evidence, best ignored or refuted by other evidence or comment, may be inflated by inept cross-examination. But some secondary facts may be valuable circumstantial evidence, clues to whether an event occurred, or signs of credibility. Cross-examination on such facts may have an effect out of proportion to the significance of each fact by itself.

Cross-examination on really strong evidence may be pointless or harmful. If the evidence is accurate, cross-examination is not designed to destroy it; it may just be emphasized.

To cross-examine a really adverse and determined witness point by point, may only increase the damage by adding detail, elaboration, repetition and emphasis. If such a cross-examination continues, without impact on the witness, it may degenerate into pointless assertion or counter-assertion, which is of no help.

But at times, where the witness rejects everything put to him, the cumulative effect of denials which are obviously unreasonable may discredit him.

One method, often used by prosecutors, is to put the contrary version of facts in one comprehensive question, with which the witness can only disagree to a limited extent.

If destructive cross-examination is not making any impact on the witness or his evidence, it will be less harmful to the cross-examiner's case if it is ended at once, unless, of course, the cross-examination is then directed to some other topic.

(b) Challenging the witness

A cross-examiner will decide whether to treat a witness as (a) mistaken, or (b) untruthful, and ought to be consistent about this.

If *mistake* is alleged, a conscientious witness may concede some doubt and that he is possibly mistaken. Otherwise some persuasion may be tried, with or without success. A stark suggestion to the witness that he is mistaken, without laying a foundation for it, is unlikely to be accepted, or to impress magistrates.

Even honest witnesses may resist criticism of their evidence, from bias, partisanship, vanity, fear of inconsistency or of seeming to have poor powers of observation or a bad memory.

Perhaps the most common suggestions of mistake refer to visual identification or passing forms of conduct which leave no trace.

The sources of errors in observation and memory are surveyed in the next chapter. But even if these are detected, it does not follow inevitably that evidence is mistaken or unreliable.

Mental states affecting the accuracy of evidence, such as the attention paid to the event; how it was observed; and the effect of discussion on recall, are hard to judge. The task of magistrates will be simpler if a cross-examiner has elicited objective facts from which such matters may be inferred.

A key to this issue is that if a witness is trusted, his own assessment of the accuracy of his observations and memory may be very significant. If magistrates have confidence in a witness, his assurance that the facts were as he states, may overcome doubts about any difficulties of observation or recall. But experience has shown that sincerity by itself is no guarantee of accuracy, particularly in visual identification.

In challenging a witness as *untruthful* a cross-examiner may focus on his character and motives.

For magistrates, bare personal details, such as age, marital status or occupation, while part of the picture, are hardly a basis for a view of character in relation to credibility.

The scope for exposing bad character in cross-examination is restricted.

An accused's criminal record is protected against disclosure, unless he loses his shield under statutory exceptions. Defence witnesses may be cross-examined as to bad character and previous convictions, but not for vexatious purposes. In any event, while a witness's proved bad character may create general distrust, its link with telling the truth or not in the particular trial situation may be a matter of doubt. A better guide to lie-detection than general character is motivation in the particular situation.

In challenging a witness as untruthful on personal grounds, cross-examination will focus on his motives in his particular situation. This is discussed in Chapter 7. Here, it suffices to say that to hope for a conviction or an acquittal does not, in itself, mean that a witness will lie to achieve it. A good illustration is that an accused's strong desire for acquittal does not show whether he is telling the truth or not. But motive is a fact to be taken into account in assessing evidence.

A cross-examiner may ask a witness about his motives. Denials often lack the ring of truth. Facts may be extracted to show his links with the parties or the issues – relationship to the accused, an interest in compensation, or a complaint against a police witness. If such facts are material but were not disclosed in examination-in-chief, this will reflect on the opponent's case, or the witness, depending on how he was questioned then.

Independent witnesses — those with no apparent interest in the case — tend to have good status, since they have no reason to lie. But cross-examination may sometimes reveal unsuspected motives which could lead to deception, perhaps about secondary facts.

Cross-examination about character or motives is unlikely, alone, to expose lying — or to reveal the truth. But it may create distrust of the witness. If so, the effect will vary with the circumstances, thus distrust of a prosecution witness to an essential fact would be serious.

Distrust of a witness is most destructive when cross-examination also creates doubt in his evidence by exposing objective flaws in it. This dual attack may be decisive.

How a witness is motivated, and how this had led him into false testimony, usually emerges in cross-examination about the issues, rather than about his credit. His turns, twists and distortions, in evidence of the essential facts, may then leave no doubt about his falsehood.

At some point a cross-examiner may suggest explicitly to the witness that he is lying. If he does this prematurely, or without laying a foundation, it may have no impact.

He ought not to accuse the witness of lying without reasonable grounds in his instructions. But it is poor advocacy to suggest that a witness who must know the facts is mistaken, where his inaccuracy could only be due to lying.

Advocates often do this. Some may think that it is diplomatic, good style, or that it will lead a witness to co-operate. But for the court, this practice may damage the cross-examiner's case. It is patently insincere. It seems half-hearted and may arise from lack of confidence, or reluctance to offend an honest witness. Moreover, it misdirects the court's attention to the wrong set of factors, that is, those which cause mistakes,not those which lead to lying.

(c) Challenging the evidence: inconsistency

The real aim of destructive cross-examination is to contradict facts; criticizing witnesses is incidental. Distrust in a witness is created only to support the attack on his account of the facts.

To be believed, evidence must be reasonable. The aim in challenging evidence is to show that it is unreasonable, and, specifically, that it is inconsistent or improbable or both.

Inconsistent statements are those which cannot be true together, for example, that at a specified time, a window was, and was not, broken. As a matter of logic, one or other of these statements must be rejected. Inconsistency does not show which statement should be accepted and which rejected. As a matter of fact, both statements may be untrue.

Inconsistency may arise within the evidence of one witness, or in comparing the evidence of two or more witnesses who support the same version of the facts, and who usually, but not necessarily, are called by the same party.

In this book, the word "inconsistency" is used to refer only to a conflict of evidence within one version of the facts; and the word "contradiction" refers to a conflict of evidence between opposing versions of the facts, which are usually, but not necessarily, given by witnesses on opposite sides — the normal clash of eyewitness evidence between prosecution and defence witnesses. The reason for the above qualification, "not necessarily", is that occasionally a prosecution witness may support the defence story, or *vice versa*.

Inconsistency does not establish any facts or destroy any particular piece of evidence. It only shows that some part of it is incorrect and must be either mistaken or untrue, thus preparing the ground for the court's acceptance of contradictory evidence called by the cross-examiner.

A cross-examiner will focus on any inconsistency which emerged in the examination-in-chief, and where he can, he will lead a witness or witnesses into further inconsistency. He will then try to exploit this to create the maximum damage.

Cross-examiners can usually find minor discrepancies in the opponent's evidence, which arise from the normal fallibility of observation and memory, and may hardly matter. Magistrates should be alert to the tendency to exaggerate them and to argue that evidence is therefore unreliable or untruthful. Such unimportant discrepancies should, of course, be distinguished from those found in secondary but significant facts which count as circumstantial evidence, or which are important clues to credibility, such as the television programme which was seen by witnesses to an alibi.

Material inconsistency about or relating to essential facts, that is, the commission of the crime or the identification of the accused, can be very damaging to the case of the party who depends on that evidence, especially if that party is the prosecution, because of the burden of proof.

If inconsistency seems to have arisen from an honest mistake, the damage may be limited to the area of evidence where it is found, without discrediting any witness – unless a cross-examiner exploits unreasonable dogmatism so as to demonstrate that the witness is generally unreliable, thus affecting his other evidence.

Where inconsistency suggests lying, the damage is greater. If one or more witnesses tell a similar story but disagree about important facts which they must know, any or all of them may be distrusted. A cross-examiner may be expected to develop this; he can often shake or shatter the court's confidence in the evidence, extending the effect beyond the immediate area of inconsistency.

Obvious inconsistency is easily challenged. But even where it is not apparent, it may be created in a lying witness. By challenging him directly and firmly and confronting him with adverse points, he may be driven beyond his prepared story into invention. When forced to amplify false evidence in various directions further flaws may emerge. The witness may be kept off balance by rapid and unexpected questions in random sequence, with little time to think or recall what he said before.

This can be done with one or more witnesses until their evidence diverges seriously. What one said may be put to another. None may see the overall aim. The cumulative effect may be compelling.

Once inconsistency emerges, the cross-examiner may exploit it in several ways.

If the cross-examination is ended at once, the witness has no chance to reconcile or correct inconsistencies (although the opponent may attempt this in re-examination). On the other hand, the cross-examiner may give the witness every chance to explain the inconsistencies, knowing that either he will be unable to do so, or may try to do so by changing his evidence. Either result would increase the damage.

In the cross-examiner's closing speech, inconsistency in his opponent's evidence is vulnerable to attack.

Inconsistent evidence in court is not unrelated to a witness's previous out-of-court statement which is inconsistent with his testimony. If the witness denies the previous statement which is put to him, it can be proved by evidence. This powerful tactic of cross-examination often leads lying and anxious witnesses to admit that they made the statement, and sometimes, its truth. Unless they do so, the previous statement is only admissible to discredit the witness in court; it is not evidence of its contents.

The consistency of a body of evidence may have the effect of increasing its weight and the likelihood that it is true.

But excessive consistency may sometimes suggest that witnesses have fabricated their evidence in collusion.

There is no instant test for distinguishing one of these conditions of evidence from the other. Dubious testimony will be probed by advocates.

A cross-examiner will focus on, and magistrates should note, unnatural consistency in the evidence of several witnesses, such as the use of identical language, phrases, topics, sequence of evidence, or items remembered or forgotten. They may be made to repeat their evidence so that its similarity and parrot-like quality becomes obvious.

If the testimony to be given by a witness will assert something impossible, it will usually be corrected or eliminated in the course of preparing for the trial. If it survives the elimination process, into the trial, it is likely to be rejected as repugnant to common sense. This topic needs no elaboration here.

(d) Challenging the evidence: improbability

Acceptable evidence must also pass the other great test – the probability that the facts are as stated. This is central to fact-finding, and a fertile area for cross-examination.

Issues of probability pervade most criminal trials. This does not imply any departure from the standard of proof beyond reasonable doubt which is required for conviction. That is the final ground of decision. Here, the probability of single facts is the issue.

The ultimate nature of probability may be left to mathematicians and philosophers. Its negative aspect, improbability, is discussed here for practical purposes, as a defect in evidence. In simple everyday terms, the test is whether or not the reported facts are likely to have occurred. This is always a matter of degree. The facts alleged may range from likely to absurd and will arouse belief or disbelief accordingly.

The evaluation of probability is a practical judgment based on common sense, experience of life, and, to some extent, intuition. It has no rules. It is certainly not a matter of law and it is appropriate for lay justices to make such decisions.

Questions of mathematical probability are usually confined to technical evidence, as in some drink and driving charges. In practice, questions of improbability usually relate to human nature linked to the conduct of the accused and others involved in the event, and sometimes witnesses also.

A cross-examiner will try to show that evidence is improbable, by probing and expanding the surrounding facts. Facts do not exist in a vacuum. They are linked with other facts which happened before, together with, or after them.

Facts may be seen as improbable to the extent that they do not fit into this context. The cross-examiner will increase the contact of the evidence with reality to expose as many points as possible where this fit breaks down, and the evidence does not correspond with other facts.

The greater the number and variety of facts, the better the chance of finding a ground for rejecting the challenged evidence as improbable. On the other hand, if the attempt fails, it will tend to set up the validity of the evidence which it set out to destroy.

An advocate will assemble the improbable elements in the opponent's evidence and will argue that the story as a whole is incredible.

Such persuasion rarely takes the form of a wholly logical argument. The conclusions are seldom inevitable. With some subtle rhetoric, the bench may be asked to compare the challenged facts with everyday experience.

So far, this account of improbability has referred to eye-witness evidence. But the question may also arise in connection with opinion or impression evidence and circumstantial evidence.

In opinion evidence, an expert witness often infers his conclusion from facts, with a greater or lesser degree of probability.

In the impression evidence of a lay witness, if this is admitted, he will reach a conclusion by interpreting what he observed.

In each case, in the ways explained previously, a cross-examiner will try to alter the witnesses' inferences, which will involve shifts in their views of the probability of their conclusions.

In circumstantial evidence, the court, not the witness, makes the inference from the facts. An advocate who hopes for a particular conclusion must depend on argument, not cross-examination, unless he challenges the underlying facts or leads evidence to support his main contentions.

Chapter 6

Detecting mistakes

Trust in honest witnesses is the basis of our system of justice. But courts must guard against inaccuracy caused by imperfect observation and memory. They must take care not to accept mistaken evidence; not to reject accurate evidence, and to avoid forming an unsound impression on incomplete evidence which is accurate, but edited.

The "reliability" of evidence means the extent to which it is acceptable as accurate and free from mistakes. The "credibility" of evidence means the extent to which it is acceptable as truthful, and is discussed in the next chapter. Mistakes are unintentional. No offence is committed by testifying inaccurately in good faith. Mistakes cannot be eliminated by law, but may be reduced by some rules and procedures. Cross-examination plays a vital part in exposing mistakes in evidence, and in showing the limits of accuracy. Another check against mistaken evidence is comparing the evidence of witnesses – although several can err about the same fact, as in visual identification.

For guidance in detecting mistakes in observation or memory, courts need to know how they arise.

Mistakes of observation arise out of (1) the subject of the observation; (2) the conditions of observation; and (3) the state of the witness.

1. The subject observed

The time available for observation depends on the duration, repetition and frequency of the event. The actual time spent in observing does not necessarily determine accuracy. That a hut is on fire can be seen in a flash; suspicious conduct of youths near it may take longer to grasp.

But an event of any duration is only an *opportunity* to observe. *Actual* observation depends on sufficient attention to the facts. A driver distracted by conversation may not see a pedestrian on the road, however long the pedestrian was visible. Similarly, a lengthy opportunity of seeing an offender does not by itself guarantee correct recognition if little attention was paid to him.

Estimates of the passing of time are seldom reliable. Stress may make an event seem longer.

In cross-examination it is difficult to overcome a witness's insistence that he had enough time to see what he reports. But too much detail or dogmatism may be suspect where there was only time for a fleeting glance.

Reports about a moving subject, such as a person or a motor car, raise problems of brief exposure, possibly complicated by obstruction of the witness's view. A typical risk of confused observation may arise in police evidence about a disorderly group. It might seem odd if one officer was able to focus attention on all of them, or if by chance, or arrangement, several officers had focused attention on every accused. A mere impression that "they were all in it" may be dangerous.

Whatever elements may be visible in any event, what counts is what is watched, and that cannot be assumed to be the important facts.

Attention, whether it is spontaneous or deliberate, is always selective. Some facts stand out naturally and rob others of attention. Urgent concerns may dominate; for example, a brandished knife, so that the assailant's face is ignored. Novel or unusual facts may attract disproportionate attention.

Cross-examination may draw out exactly what concerned a witness most in the event. It may be suggested that he cannot testify properly to other or peripheral matters, and has filled in gaps in his story from imagination or as a result of discussion with other witnesses.

A violent event may cause stress to observers, but unless they become disorientated, they may report it accurately, as many do.

Ambiguity in the event – two possible meanings for the same facts – may be a problem, for example, whether an adult touched a child at all or did so accidentally, affectionately, or indecently.

Ambiguity may arise in evidence of an impression which is admissible as the only way of conveying what the witness saw. A cross-examiner is likely to probe its factual basis.

Ambiguity in recollection or language may occur if recognition is confused with resemblance. In recognition, the witness is saying "that is the man". If this is accepted, identity is proved. In resemblance, the witness is saying "that looks like the man". If this is accepted, it does not prove identity by itself; it is only an item of circumstantial evidence. It is essential to eliminate such ambiguity.

Evidence may be obscure rather than ambiguous, as where the witness is uncertain about what he *saw*, rather than about what it meant.

Even honest witnesses are often uncertain or mistaken in evidence of intangible or abstract facts, such as the duration of an event, dates, times, the sequence of facts, distances, layout, dimensions, the relationship of things to each other, weights, quantities, colours or speed. Witnesses usually state subjective views which tend to support their main evidence.

Sometimes evidence of objective facts can help the court to assess the accuracy of evidence of intangible or abstract facts. But reports of such facts are often beyond testing. If precision is crucial, great care is needed in deciding such facts. Trust or distrust in witnesses and their stated degrees of confidence are likely to be important. Moreover, evidence of any kind should be assessed in the context of the whole of the evidence in the trial.

2. Conditions of observation

Apart from features of the event which can mar observation, the surrounding conditions may affect the observer and make his evidence incomplete or inaccurate.

Objections to the reliability of the evidence on these grounds, usually emerge for the first time in cross-examination. It is unlikely that adverse conditions of observation will be referred to in the evidence-in-chief.

Witnesses who give firm evidence about the event may be slow to concede that they could not observe it clearly because of the conditions of observation, but sometimes their insistence may be contradicted by other evidence, possibly of an objective kind.

The quality of lighting is a common issue. Crimes often occur, and offenders are then seen (if at all) in darkness. Questions may arise about the location and strength of artificial lighting. In a dispute about whether visual identification is mistaken, the quality of the lighting may be crucial.

The state of the weather – rain, snow, mist, fog, dazzling sunshine, or wet windows, windscreens or spectacles – may interfere with observation. Again, eyewitnesses may be reluctant to accept this.

The witness's distance from the incident is a common issue. If he was too far away to see everything properly, he may have filled in the gaps by speculation or as the result of discussion.

Again, positive eyewitnesses are unlikely to accept this objection. Estimates of such distances are notoriously subjective and variable, yet objective evidence is uncommon.

Witnesses who claim that they saw something are unlikely to agree that they could not do so because of a visual obstruction, such as a tree or a lorry. Objective evidence of the layout, and of the obstruction, will help.

Distractions may divert an eyewitness's attention from the event described. If this is denied, evidence that a distraction was there, does not alone determine how it affected the witness.

Generally, the conditions of observation are likely to arise in examination-in-chief only if they were favourable. A witness who testified positively is likely to resist such objections to reliability, and much may depend on the court's trust in a confident witness.

3. The state of the witness

The completeness and accuracy of evidence may be affected by the state of the witness, that is, his permanent abilities and any temporary bodily or mental condition. Permanent abilities include the quality of vision and hearing, which is usually taken to be normal. If specific defects emerge, their role in the reliability of the observation would be relevant. Temporary bodily states often encountered arise from injury, illness, fatigue, drugs or alcohol.

Injury may interfere with perception directly, as where blood flows into a victim's eyes from a head wound; or it may simply distract his attention. The nature and location of a victim's wounds may indicate that he was unable to see his assailant at the moment of attack, for example, where he suffered multiple bruises on his body and arms, but not on his head, suggesting that he shielded his face with his hands.

Alcohol may reduce the quality of perception, but its effect is complex and depends on many factors. Its effect is often exaggerated, and may only justify caution, not rejection of the evidence so affected.

Prolonged cross-examination about the details of drinking over a period will not be scientific proof of impaired observation. Unknown factors would include the witness's metabolism, physique, and his intake of food. A positive witness is unlikely to undermine his evidence by accepting that it is unreliable or mistaken for this reason.

The effect of impairment due to drink may depend on what is observed. The facts are often so stark that, even after heavy drinking, a witness may have no problem in observing them.

By itself, a witness's admission that he had been drinking is usually seen as colouring his reliability, rather than as a reason to reject his evidence, apart from extreme cases. But if there are other reasons to suspect his evidence, drink may add to the doubts.

An important effect of drink is that it may affect memory, but that is a different matter from impaired observation.

What a witness expects to see at the time is a temporary mental state which can create errors. For example, a flickering shadow on a window, cast by a tree waving in the wind, may appear to an anxious person alone at home, to be the face of the Peeping Tom neighbour.

Some temporary mental states, of course, may develop from persistent preconceived ideas which are more or less permanent.

Psychology shows that perception of even a simple fact involves more than visual sensation. The brain builds sensations into patterns and wholes and gives them a meaning. Thus, expectations arising from past experience can lead to misinterpretation of facts, as where a store detective perceives everyone who handles goods to be acting suspiciously.

Attention is a temporary mental state which is significant for accuracy. It has a limited span in time and place; it moves from one thing to another, selecting its target naturally or at will.

Thus, some facts (hearing a window being smashed) may be perceived clearly; some facts (the television programme at the time) may be noted only vaguely; and other facts (what a neighbour shouted) may go unnoticed.

The main facts may stand out and reduce the attention

given to secondary facts. Mistakes may occur if a witness completes the picture from imagination or interpretation and reports everything as if he had perceived it clearly.

Stress in witnesses to a disturbing incident is unlikely to impair their observations unless it is so intense as to cause hysteria or disorientation. Eyewitness evidence of violent incidents is accepted regularly.

Where the facts are intangible, vague, rapid or ambiguous, errors which arise from the mental state of witnesses are more likely.

Conduct-crimes, having no result, may consist of brief and fleeting behaviour, as in the case of indecent exposure in a park. An anxious individual who expects this may, sincerely but wrongly misinterpret an incident.

Evidence of an attempt to commit a result-crime may be no more than suspicion about an innocent act, for example, if the accused heard glass breaking, entered an absent neighbour's garden to check the windows, intending to call the police, and was seen by another neighbour as the culprit who was acting suspiciously.

Evidence of visual identification is vulnerable to mistakes caused by a witness's state of mind, for example, if he expects the offender to be in an identification parade although warned against it. Again, a witness, thinking that the police must be right, may convert resemblance into recognition, without realizing it.

The more that facts are uncertain, obscure or ambiguous, the greater the risk that a witness's attitude may distort his observations. But where obvious facts are easily observable, the witness's attitude is unlikely to create mistakes or affect his testimony.

It is difficult to challenge evidence of observation as mistaken because of the witness's state of mind. A cross-examiner would need to establish the unrealized influence, and that it caused a mistake, which the witness will not accept.

Where such a suggestion is supported by objective facts, it may have a good prospect of acceptance by the court, despite the witness's denial, for example, attention will be focused on a hail of stones rather than on trying to identify the assailants.

That conclusion can be reached by inference, even if the victims of the attack insist that their identifications were made at the time, and were accurate. But the special feature here is that the salient facts had such personal urgency that there could be no doubt what received attention in the situation.

4. Memory

In fact-finding, courts rely on the memory of honest witnesses. Generally, it is sound for essential facts but less so for secondary facts. The fallibility of memory must be accepted. Courts must always bear in mind that the evidence of even trusted witnesses, may be incomplete or inaccurate in some ways. Again, a witness whose memory of the event is accurate, may, by lack of confidence in it, create unnecessary doubt.

The reliability of a witness's memory is always open to challenge in cross-examination, but while this may weaken evidence, it is rarely conclusive unless it is supported by something else, such as contradictory evidence.

No matter how good observation of an event was, the memory of it will fade with time. Psychologists say that forgetting happens rapidly at first and then slows down, but they disagree about whether this holds for facial recognition. Most people can remember familiar faces, not seen for decades. No rules about forgetting exist which can replace practical judgment in particular circumstances.

Long delays between the offence and the trial are inevitable. In regard to the fading of memory, what weight a court should give to the interval of time will depend on the situation.

But this is only one factor; in isolation, it can hardly determine the reliability of a given item of evidence. Other factors include a wide range of individual dif-

ferences in memory, the clarity of the original observation, its significance for the witness, reinforcement of
the memory image by later repetition, and so on.

Forgetting can range from a mere dimming of memory, so
that it becomes less vivid, to total amnesia for facts,
incidents and faces. Studies show that, as common sense
suggests, the main facts tend to resist forgetting more
than secondary details. One might expect the nature and
meaning of a crime to remain clearly enough in memory,
while minor facts gradually vanish. This may not matter
unless the minor facts were important steps in
circumstantial evidence or clues to credibility.

Forgotten details lead to minor discrepancies between
witnesses, the importance of which should not be
exaggerated.

Psychologists disagree about how delay affects facial
recognition. The common-sense expectation would be that
long delay would create a danger of misidentification.
Whether or not the witness was familiar with the person
identified, would be important. If he was familiar with
him, he would be recalling personal identity with its
associations, rather than a face. This might reduce or
remove the risk.

It is to be expected that a witness who gives firm evidence
of any kind will deny a suggestion that, because of the
delay, he has forgotten the facts and is mistaken about
them. But magistrates will know the extent of the delay,
and will give such weight to the passage of time as seems
proper, in the context of the whole of the evidence.

5. Suggestion

A weak memory caused by poor observation, or fading,
may be influenced by suggestion – the uncritical
acceptance and assimilation of an idea, simply because it
is presented.

The meaning of an event may be changed by suggestion.
A new image may be formed which is a compromise
between the real memory and the added material. This

image may include facts which did not exist, or exclude those which did. The witness, believing that this is his genuine memory, testifies sincerely and convincingly.

But this is not inevitable. To the extent that observation was good, and memory is clear and firm, it will tend to resist suggestion. Also, memory for essential facts is less suggestible than memory for secondary facts. Often, only details in evidence are affected by suggestion.

Witnesses can easily be influenced by investigations, and later, by preparations for the trial. The police, in early informal enquiries, may welcome any scraps of information which could help them to trace a suspect, and may elicit hearsay, opinion, or even guesses for practical purposes, which witnesses interviewed may absorb. This can also happen in the defence preparations for trial. It is recognized that something may be injected into a witness's written statement without its being intended or realized. This may happen more than once.

Discussion of some unusual or dramatic event between witnesses is natural, and inevitable if they meet, as they will if they are relatives, friends or workmates. It is not unlawful unless it is done to falsify evidence. The effect may be to streamline evidence and to make it more complete and more consistent than it would have been.

Many witnesses are reluctant to admit any discussion of evidence, and it would be exceptional for any witness to concede that it had influenced his evidence. This is an opening for effective cross-examination to cast doubt on witnesses' explanations.

But, apart from suggestion by other persons, self-induced changes in memory of the event may occur, which can lead to mistaken evidence.

This process may be conscious, as in rehearsing and streamlining evidence, reconciling inconsistencies, or completing gaps by imagination or inference.

Changes in memory may also arise without its being realized, from internal processes such as emotions, motives, wishes, anxieties, vanity, desire to help the police, or fear of embarrassment.

Over a period, such processes may bend a witness's memory of the event one way or another, so that mistakes are introduced. These are probably universal tendencies. But while they may colour the evidence of honest witnesses, it would be generally accepted that their reports of essential facts are unlikely to be affected. Usually it is the peripheral facts which are vulnerable to such distortions.

It is generally impossible for cross-examination to expose the subtle effects of suggestion with any compelling effect. But magistrates may have such matters in mind in reaching their decisions.

6. Mistaken evidence of identity

A common issue is whether or not it was the accused who committed the crime. He may be incriminated by visual identification, circumstantial evidence, or a confession.

Like any type of evidence, these three forms are liable to mistakes in observation or memory in the ways discussed above. But in addition, evidence of visual identification needs special consideration. If it is the real issue, it is of crucial importance. Also, it is generally accepted that visual identification is fallible.

A court must exercise special care before convicting on such evidence. In 1976 a committee headed by Lord Devlin concluded that " . . . in cases which depend wholly or mainly on eyewitness evidence of identification there is a special risk of wrong conviction. It arises because the value of such evidence is exceptionally difficult to assess; the witness who has sincerely convinced himself and whose sincerity carries conviction is not infrequently mistaken."

Guidelines laid down in the 1977 case of *Turnbull* apply to cases which depend wholly or substantially on the accuracy of visual identification, contested as mistaken by the defence. *Turnbull* should be consulted for details of the risks which courts must consider, and the tests which they must apply.

The Devlin Report distinguished three forms of visual identification: recognition; resemblance; and distinctive characteristics.

Recognition is the strongest form of identification. Here the witness asserts that he recognizes the accused as the offender. If this is accepted, identity is proved.

For the witness, the subjective test is the sense of familiarity which he feels on matching the accused's face with the recalled image of the offender's face. Unfortunately this sense of familiarity is sometimes caused by seeing the accused elsewhere than in the act of committing the crime. Clearly, such a subjective experience could sometimes be mistaken, and although the witness states his degree of confidence in his identification, it can be very hard to support, to challenge, or to evaluate.

If the witness knew the accused at the time of the crime, his identification could still be mistaken because of the flaws in observation and memory discussed earlier.

Where prosecution witnesses claim that their identifications are accurate, the defence will try to weaken them by raising a reasonable doubt, or by leading contradictory evidence.

Evidence of *resemblance* means that the accused's appearance is similar to that of the offender. Even if this is accepted, it proves nothing by itself. It may be true even if the accused was unconnected with the crime. Resemblance is only an item of circumstantial evidence for evaluation with the other evidence.

It is essential that evidence of recognition be distinguished from evidence of resemblance. Questions or answers should not be allowed to confuse these two forms of visual identification. Sometimes witnesses vacillate between one and the other and great care on the part of the court is necessary.

Evidence of resemblance contains a built-in element of doubt. The witness, having seen the offender, cannot say that the accused is that person, despite the likeness.

Evidence of resemblance is liable to the same kind of mistakes as evidence of recognition, *viz* the subjectivity of the comparison, the possibility that the feeling of familiarity arises from seeing the accused elsewhere than in the act of committing the crime, and any of the other sources of error which can affect observation or memory.

The defence may dispute an alleged resemblance by reference to details of appearance, or they may accept that the resemblance exists, while highlighting the fact that, nevertheless, the accused is not recognizable as the offender. The aim would be to raise a reasonable doubt. In addition the defence might try to nullify the circumstantial value of the resemblance for the prosecution by means of exonerating evidence.

A witness may say that the offender and the accused have some *special feature* in common, a scar or a missing tooth, perhaps. The value of the comparison depends on how common or unusual that feature is. A tattoo with the same six-digit number on the forearms of the offender and the accused, would obviously count for more than having blue eyes in common. Unless it is more or less unique, for example a distinctive birthmark, a special feature is just an item of circumstantial evidence and is not compelling in itself. In such evidence, the original observation of the feature on the offender may have been mistaken, or the similarity to the feature seen on the accused, may be exaggerated.

Visual identification evidence, whether in the form of recognition, resemblance or comparison of some distinctive characteristic, may be liable to mistake which arises from pre-trial police procedures for the identification of suspects. While these procedures may help police enquiries, they may interfere with accurate identification later.

One such practice is that police obtain descriptions of the suspect from witnesses. Such descriptions, as verbal labels, may mislead a witness in a later identification, or he may be influenced by them into identifying a suspect who matches the description. The defence ought to obtain a copy of any description for comparison with the accused.

Later mistakes in identification could also arise where the police have shown photographs of suspects to witnesses, or have arranged informal confrontations between witnesses and suspects.

While police practice regulates, but discourages, these methods, they are sometimes necessary in urgent circumstances. The danger is the entry of suggestive elements under informal and uncontrolled circumstances.

The preferred method is an identification parade held under strictly regulated conditions. The rules are intended to ensure fairness and to exclude any suggestive elements which could lead to misidentification.

On the view that seeing the accused in the dock may incline a witness to identify him wrongly, an identification of the accused for the first time, in court, may be thought less reliable than one which confirms an earlier identification.

Visual identification evidence may be supported by circumstantial evidence, that is, facts from which the accused's identity as the offender may be inferred – or the identification evidence may be wholly circumstantial. The combination of secondary facts may create a meaningful pattern which incriminates the accused beyond reasonable doubt. These facts might include the accused's motives; conduct before and after the crime; traces on the victim, the scene or on himself, linking him to the crime; or incriminating articles found in his possession.

Chapter 7

The lying witness

Everyday conversation, where a need or wish to deceive may be weak is, nevertheless, often tainted by deception ranging from mild fibs to pure inventions. In criminal trials, where motives are strong, false evidence is common.

Unreliable or mistaken evidence was considered in the previous chapter. The credibility of evidence, to be discussed now, is the extent to which evidence is acceptable as truthful.

Lies and mistakes should be clearly distinguished. A lie is an inaccurate statement made with intent to deceive. A mistaken statement is inaccurate but without that intent. A witness who knows facts but reports them inaccurately does so intentionally and is lying.

Deciding the credibility of evidence is the main problem in criminal trials. It must be done correctly. Miscarriages of justice may follow from believing a lie, disbelieving the truth, doubting what should be sure, or being sure of what should be doubted.

Lying is a psychological process. It might be thought that psychology could offer help in lie detection. Unfortunately, it cannot do so. In almost 100 years of massive research into testimony, psychologists have virtually ignored lying; their methodology only allowed them to study mistakes in observation or memory. Belated research in recent years into bodily signs of lying has had no practical results.

There is no known psychological method for penetrating a liar's mind − apart from hypnosis. Psychologists have no advantage over other persons in judging whether or not someone is telling the truth. No psychological findings can help courts to detect lying.

1. Credibility

Instead of evaluating credibility from an individual's evidence, a criminal trial is designed to present the whole picture, and to allow for analysis and comparison of testimonies. It is thus a unique way of discovering the truth.

Advocates may lead any relevant evidence. Witnesses testify and submit to challenge in cross-examination. Although advocates must not mislead the court knowingly, their partiality in challenging evidence can help the court in assessing it.

The whole body of evidence from different sources is tested from various angles and analysed for consistency and probability and compared for contradiction. Rules about the burden and standard of proof are applied in reaching a decision. A court should use all the approaches open to it. Belief in some evidence may establish trustworthy facts as a context for assessing other doubtful evidence. Plausible evidence may be rejected because it clashes with accepted evidence. This is one key to deciding credibility. It is essential to keep the whole picture in mind.

Lying cannot be eliminated by law. It can only be discouraged, exposed if possible, and punished when it is detected. Many witnesses are determined to lie from motives which are strong enough to overcome the deterrents and the risks. Lying occurs despite the oath and penalties for perjury or offences related to witnesses. Witnesses are rarely prosecuted for perjury. It may be undetected, or difficult or impossible to prove. A prosecution would involve another trial, which would largely duplicate the one in which the perjury is alleged to have occurred. Also, not all forms of deception are perjury.

Some rules of law, such as that allowing reference to previous inconsistent statements, are designed to reduce the effects of lying. But essentially, how credibility is decided is beyond legal regulation.

The credibility of evidence can be decided only by applying common sense and practical judgment based on experience.

No judges, barristers, solicitors, psychologists or experts have any specialist knowledge about credibility which is superior to lay judgment. This is recognized by the system of lay justice which prevails almost universally in magistrates' courts and in the trial of serious crimes by lay jurors.

This does not mean that skill in assessing credibility cannot be improved by practical training and experience.

2. Forms of lying

Dishonest forms of evidence range from omissions or subtle twists, to gross inventions. It is easier to detect deception if one is familiar with the main forms which it takes – false assertions or denials, false colouring, evasiveness, and omissions.

(a) False assertions or denials

The most blatant kind of lying falls into the danger zone of perjury. It consists of definite statements which assert an invented fact, such as a false alibi; or deny a real fact, for example, that the accused was at the scene of the crime.

Such stark lies involve double motives, *viz* the original reason for lying, and then fear of the penalties for exposure.

Witnesses who lie in this way are unlikely to retract their false evidence and confess the truth, even under forceful cross-examination. Their motives are generally too strong for that. But magistrates should be alert for the emergence of defects which weaken that evidence, so that it is finally overcome by contradictory evidence which is believed.

(b) False colouring

Some subtle forms of deceit fall short of false assertions or denials. They are more or less true statements which have been twisted intentionally to give them a desired slant.

The door is always open to half-truths. Witnesses, in their own language, are free to describe facts in variable ways. Impression evidence may be the only way of reporting ambiguous or obscure facts, such as suspicious behaviour in a supermarket, erratic driving, or sexually dubious conduct. A dishonest witness may exploit the vagueness of such events by deliberate misinterpretation.

Words of doubt or confidence may qualify evidence quite sincerely. But an insincere witness may profess doubt where he is sure, or certainty where he is unsure. He may undermine the effect of evidence by stressing difficulties of observation or memory, or he may exaggerate his confidence on spurious grounds. Such colouring of evidence should be probed to see if it is genuine or not.

Witnesses who only colour their evidence are not motivated strongly enough for perjury. If cross-examination shows that there is no factual basis for the way in which they are bending the evidence, they may perhaps have to correct this. But if they seem to resist this unreasonably, the colouring may be disregarded.

(c) Evasiveness

For various reasons, few people are keen to testify; reluctant witnesses are not a special class. Mild reluctance may cause a lack of co-operation, although, when pressed, the witness gives evidence truthfully, albeit with some hesitation. Stronger reluctance may produce various degrees of evasiveness which are a form of deception.

Evasive witnesses usually stop short of perjury. Evasiveness would spoil an invented story. Also, the risk of penalties may deter these weakly motivated witnesses. They rarely refuse to answer questions at all, although some, caught in a dilemma, may break down and become inarticulate.

Such witnesses may fence with questions by avoiding the real point or by giving ambiguous or obscure answers. They may claim that they did not see, or that they have forgotten, an incident. Their amnesia for some facts but excellent memory for others, may be suspect.

Evasiveness is common in prosecution witnesses who withdraw previous complaints, such as victims of domestic violence who become reconciled with the offender.

Evasiveness is usually obvious and may lead to warnings. With the court's leave, an advocate may treat his own witness as hostile, and may cross-examine him. A witness may be referred to his previous inconsistent statements; if he is afraid to deviate from them too obviously, he may be coaxed into giving complete and truthful evidence.

(d) Omissions

Whether or not an omission of material facts from an answer is perjury, partly depends on the form of the question. A witness is bound by his oath or affirmation to answer questions, not to volunteer information which may be helpful, or to report all that he knows about the facts in issue. But the narrow questions which are usually asked to avoid unpleasant surprises may not refer to some vital facts.

Usually, omitting material facts is the easiest form of dishonest testimony. There is little or nothing to prepare as a false story or to remember. The risk of telling lies is avoided. Under challenge, it might be claimed that these facts were not known or had been forgotten.

It will be harder for a witness to omit something important if questions are designed to bring all the material facts within their scope, and the evidence is probed thoroughly to ensure that nothing of significance escapes the net.

A leading question which is too specific may miss its target; it could be answered literally, while omitting the fact of interest, for example, if asked whether a motor car was parked outside the house, a witness may deny this quite truthfully. But a more general question, because of its width, may close an avenue of escape; thus if the witness is asked whether any vehicle was parked outside the house, he would have to say that a lorry was parked there.

So far as possible, questions should place such a witness in the dilemma of disclosing the truth or of committing perjury. A witness who has not concealed material facts improperly will incur no risk by revealing them when obliged to do so by relevant questions. Thus, omissions which could be a form of deception can often be overcome by efficient advocacy.

Omissions may be found in evidence-in-chief or in evidence given under cross-examination.

The form of the questions may show magistrates whether material facts may have been omitted.

3. Tests of lying

The credibility of any evidence depends on whether the witness who gives it is trusted; whether the evidence is reasonable; and on whether it is confirmed or contradicted by the rest of the evidence.

Unless all these conditions are fulfilled, it is to be expected that the evidence will be disbelieved. If a witness is distrusted, even reasonable evidence may be rejected. On the other hand, unreasonable evidence is likely to be disbelieved, while trust in the witness would be overcome or destroyed. Again, even reasonable evidence given by a trusted witness may be unacceptable if it is contradicted by other evidence which is firmly accepted.

4. Trusting the witness

In judging credibility, a key question, but not the only one, is whether the witness is trusted. This is an element in belief, although it would be imprudent to decide credibility only on the basis of a "hunch" about one witness. All approaches should be used.

Trust in a witness is partly an intuitive acceptance of his or her sincerity with a gut feeling which says "yes". It is a direct response of one person to another, as occurs in all human relationships. There are no rules to ensure that this response is correct. Analysis of it would not provide any practical guidance.

But trust in a witness is not only intuitive — it is also based on thinking about personal features — personality and character, motives, and demeanour — which emerge in the trial, although psychology has neither defined nor explained these qualities.

(a) Personality

Personality, here, simply means individuality. While this must enter into the equation of credibility somewhere, in the current state of psychology it is impossible to show any relationship between personality types and veracity. Common experience shows that all kinds of persons may be truthful, or lie on occasion.

(b) Character

Character — the moral aspect of personality — whether good or bad, is a poor guide to veracity. It is difficult to form a view of it or about how it affects the sincerity of evidence. It usually matters less than the witness's motives in relation to his situation.

Witnesses cannot be divided into those of good character who are truthful, and those of bad character who are not. Veracity is not a fixed quality. Many crimes, including shop-lifting, corruption, fraud, embezzlement, drink and driving offences, and sexual offences, are committed, and then denied by people with impeccable histories. Even police officers, who ought to be of good character, are regularly attacked as liars.

Personal details about family, occupation, or previous criminal convictions, are of little help. Experience shows that almost anyone may lie or not, regardless of status or past history.

(c) Motives

A motive is a state of arousal with a specific aim – a response to a situation by action in a certain direction. In court, these directions are usually obvious even if there is only a vague impression of the witness.

Unadmitted motives can often be inferred from facts suggesting interest in the situation. If such facts were concealed in evidence-in-chief, they may be more harmful if they emerge in cross-examination.

The witness's motive may be to seek conviction, acquittal, a personal goal, or simply to comply with the oath. Truth and minor untruths may be mixed.

Motives may count for a great deal in assessing credibility, although they should not be treated as conclusive in themselves.

To illustrate this, it would be unsound to reject the alibi evidence of the accused's wife solely on the ground that, "she would say that, wouldn't she?" She *would* if the alibi is true, and she *might* if it is not, so the motive alone does not decide the question.

With no basis for the decision other than the wife's feelings, the alibi evidence may be either true or false. To know which is the case, her testimony and her motives must be assessed, not in isolation, but in the context of all the evidence.

Independent witnesses are those who appear to have no reason to falsify their evidence. Prosecutors, defence advocates and courts, tend to accept them as sincere. Generally, their evidence is only challenged or rejected as mistaken.

Disinterested witnesses may be chance observers of the main event, persons speaking of items of circumstantial evidence, or experts. They are often called by the prosecution.

But from motives which are not obvious, even this evidence may be biased or untruthful. Bias may stem from prejudices, against, for example, certain types of offender or the police; from a tendency to side with the party who called the witness; or from other reasons. Extreme bias may shade into one of the forms of deliberate deception discussed above.

Seemingly independent witnesses may have hidden reasons, such as vanity, embarrassment, fear, or dishonest hope of gain, for lying. Courts must be alert to this possibility of lying about secondary or even major facts. Cross-examination may reveal grounds for animosity or favour towards a party, or imaginative probing may expose personal aims. A witness's resistance to such disclosures or response to such challenges may be significant.

Naturally, motives aimed at conviction are seen more often in prosecution witnesses.

Police witnesses testify for the prosecution regularly, but with no special status. It is common for the defence to accuse them of lying, and they may support this by leading evidence.

This raises questions of motives sharply. Why would police officers act criminally and risk loss of career or pension and imprisonment? They would know that they might be exposed in the trial or later by further police probes, informers, confessions, or a public enquiry. Police witnesses would rarely have anything to gain by lying or reasons for hostility towards the defendant. Yet experience has shown that very grave police misconduct, which includes perjury, has occurred.

If the defence fails to suggest any motive for alleged lying by police witnesses, its challenge will lose much of its force.

The most likely explicit or implied contention is that police witnesses have exaggerated or coloured their evidence from a mistaken sense of duty, or because of some degree of malice. But there is a world of difference between such deliberate misconduct and the normal police activities of tracing and arresting suspects or gathering evidence.

A serious accusation may be that police witnesses are making up or distorting admissions by the accused to overcome deficiencies in the prosecution case, or even worse, that they were parties to a criminal conspiracy to convict the accused by planting exhibits, intimidating witnesses, and perjury.

If such challenges raise a reasonable doubt about material police evidence this can be enough for acquittal, even if the reasons for the police misconduct are unexplained. It would be enough for the defence to prove or to raise doubts about improper actions. Motives can always be inferred from actions. However, if motives can be shown, the allegations will be strengthened.

The defence often accuses complainants and accomplices or their associates of lying because they are motivated to seek the conviction of the accused.

The defence may suggest that complainants who are the alleged victims of violence are motivated by malice and are simply carrying the battle into court; this may be so where self-defence is in issue.

Complainants in sexual offences, including children, may be challenged as lying maliciously.

The defence often attacks the credibility of accomplices (using the term in a general sense and not with reference to any definite legal category). Such a challenge by the defence receives support from the caution with which such evidence has always been treated.

Accomplices may have obvious motives for lying. They may incriminate the accused falsely to obtain immunity from prosecution for themselves. Again, they may seek a lighter sentence by exaggerating the blame attached to the accused and minimising their own involvement. The defence may reinforce its challenge by also attacking the accomplice's character.

An accused has the greatest interest in acquittal and is probably the most motivated of all the witnesses. His relatives or friends, as defence witnesses, would, presumably, share this wish.

As the accused should know the truth of what he is charged with, his evidence if given, will normally be attacked as untruthful, not mistaken; his associates' testimony – often eyewitness reports of the main incident or about an alibi – is likely to be attacked on the same basis.

But the caution, which was given earlier, merits repetition and emphasis. Although a court, in assessing the evidence of defence witnesses, may take their motives for acquittal into account, this alone is not a ground for rejecting it. The accused and other defence witnesses would be similarly motivated whether their evidence was truthful or not. It is only in the context of the whole of the evidence that the weight to be given to defence evidence can be evaluated.

Some witnesses, whether called by the prosecution or the defence, although indifferent to the outcome, may have some personal reason for lying. Since the motive may be unsuspected, such lies may not be exposed. If they are minor, they may not have a material effect on the evidence.

Clearly, a witness's motive in relation to his specific situation, which is usually discernible, is a better guide to lie detection than what can be gathered about his character in a criminal trial.

In some contexts, even persons of distinction and seemingly impeccable character may lie in court or elsewhere, to save a friend, perhaps. Equally, even the worst rogue sometimes tells the truth. A court must have an open mind and not make assumptions about any class of witnesses.

It should be noted, too, that where, as often occurs, motives are mixed, any witness may be partly truthful and partly untruthful.

The discussion of motives, so far, has referred to lying. But although a witness's motives are not strong enough to cause him to lie, they may, nevertheless, create bias in his evidence to a greater or lesser degree. The exact boundary between extreme bias and lying is difficult to draw, but the distinction is between distorting facts without being aware of doing so, and doing so deliberately.

(d) Demeanour

Traditionally, a witness's demeanour is supposed to help a court to decide whether or not he is lying. Thus, appeal courts which do not re-hear the evidence are reluctant to interfere with decisions of the court which saw and heard the witnesses.

Demeanour has no firm definition. It covers everything about a witness which can be seen or heard, apart from the content of his evidence.

As witnesses take the oath, their sex, age, build, general appearance, clothing, ornaments and hair style are seen. Whatever they signify, these features will not vary with the sincerity or insincerity of the evidence.

As he answers, a witness may change his posture, move or make gestures, and his facial expressions may vary. His speech may change in audibility, rate, emphasis, pitch or fluency. Such signs may be spontaneous or at the command of a good liar or an actor. Other signs, such as some facial expressions, blushing, perspiring, turning pale, or tremors, are beyond control.

Complex patterns may be distress, illness, fainting, toilet needs, crying or loss of temper.

What are magistrates to make of all this? Can one know just by looking at and listening to a witness, whether he is telling the truth or lying? Psychology, judicial experience, and common sense all reach the same negative conclusion.

After intensive research into the question, psychologists have found no reliable signs of lying – or truthfulness.

One leading researcher summed up his work after 25 years of searching for signs of lying. "There is no sign of deceit itself – no gesture, facial expression or muscle twitch that in and of itself means that person is lying". He adds that, "Most people believe they can detect false expressions; our research has shown that most cannot" [Paul Ekman, *Telling Lies*, 1986, New York].

He finds that so far as demeanour is concerned, most liars can deceive most people most of the time. At best, signs of anxiety can sometimes be detected — but the anxiety could be due to causes other than lying.

Psychology indicates that no decision should ever be made, particularly a conviction, on the basis of a witness's demeanour alone.

A distinguished judge, Lord Devlin, regards the view that a witness's demeanour will reveal whether or not he is lying, as "over-rated". He doubts his own ability to interpret demeanour and he relies on it as little as possible.

Experience in court confirms Lord Devlin's opinion. Witnesses do not usually display any reliable signs of whether or not they are lying.

An untenable view is that lying witnesses are anxious, and truthful witnesses are confident, so that bodily signs of anxiety or confidence are a guide to credibility.

A false witness may be genuinely confident for various reasons. He may be sure of being believed or that, at least, he will not be exposed as a liar. He may not care about the outcome, as where it will not affect him personally, or where a minor sentence only is possible. His evidence is a lie, but his relaxation is real.

Again, the relaxed appearance of a false witness may be simulated. Because of good natural control or court experience, many liars can hide the signs of their anxiety.

To believe such untruthful witnesses, just because they seemed to be confident, would be a misjudgment.

On the other hand, truthful witnesses often show signs of anxiety. There can be many reasons for anxiety other than lying. Some people are naturally anxious most of the time. Courts cannot compare a witness's daily state with his demeanour while testifying.

Giving evidence is itself a cause of anxiety for many honest witnesses. They may be afraid of humiliation under cross-examination if their powers of observation or memory are criticized, or that they will be disbelieved although they are telling the truth. They may be anxious about their responsibility for the decision, or, with good reason, be anxious about what the decision may be and its consequences, for example, in terms of reprisals.

It would again be a misjudgment to disbelieve such witnesses because they appear anxious.

To rely on signs of relaxation or anxiety as a guide to credibility assumes that such signs exist, that they are detectable, and that they are caused by telling the truth or lying. This assumption is not supported by psychology, judicial experience or common sense.

Another puzzle is how signs of anxiety might correspond with specific pieces of testimony. If a liar gives some truthful evidence, but is anxious throughout, how can signs of anxiety distinguish honest from dishonest evidence?

Advocacy is of little help to courts in judging a witness's demeanour. To probe a person's forms of expression or personal reactions may seem pointless, offensive, or unfair. It is poor material for a cross-examiner. He will usually find more productive lines of enquiry.

For all these reasons, as well as the range of individual differences and the complexity of personal responses, a realistic view is that any witness's demeanour could mean anything.

Thus, it would be a bold assertion for anyone, whether lay magistrate or professional judge, to claim to be "a judge of people" with a special talent for detecting lying from visible or audible signs. Miscarriages of justice could follow from such an approach.

However, a witness's demeanour need not and indeed, cannot, be ignored altogether. People do communicate by non-verbal means — popularly known as body language — as well as verbally. In this inevitable aspect of human relationships, the transmission or reception of non-verbal signals may occur without awareness and may partly explain the intuitive trust or distrust of witnesses, which has been referred to previously. But this incidental element in the judgment would be unsafe as the sole or main ground for deciding any major issue of credibility, or for finding a defendant guilty.

Chapter 8

Detecting lies from the evidence

1. Reasonableness

Belief in any evidence depends on the triple tests of trusting the witness, judging his evidence to be reasonable, and finding that it fits in with other accepted evidence. Thus, to hold that evidence is reasonable is a step towards believing it, but, by itself, does not guarantee that it will be believed. However, unreasonable evidence could be rejected at once without having to apply other tests.

Belief or disbelief, of course, involves complex psychological processes, but an analysis for court purposes need go no further.

Related questions of law, *viz* the burden and standard of proof, are considered elsewhere.

Defects which may lead courts to conclude that evidence is unreasonable are impossibility; improbability; inconsistency; and lack of realism.

Each of these kinds of defect can exist separately, or they may be combined in the same piece of evidence.

(a) Impossibility

Impossibility means a contradiction between what is stated in evidence and a fact established by proof, formal admission, or judicial awareness.

This is a conflict between a statement and reality. It must

78

be distinguished from inconsistency which is a conflict between two statements, whatever the facts may be.

Evidence which is contradicted by facts within judicial knowledge is probably absurd, for example, a claim to recognize someone a mile away. Obvious nonsense in the evidence of any witness is likely to be eliminated in preparation and to be rare in court. Similarly, if parties know before the trial that facts will be admitted formally, they are unlikely to lead evidence which the admitted facts would destroy.

In court, facts which depend on evidence are not proved or found to be impossible until the decision stage. Then, accepting some facts is a basis for rejecting contrary evidence as impossible. Impossibility would be a defect if this conflict arose within one party's evidence; otherwise the impossibility would simply follow from the defeat of one case by the other.

(b) Inconsistency

Inconsistency in evidence refers to a conflict between two statements, whatever the underlying facts may be, for example, to say that at noon the accused was at home, and to say later that he was in a pub then. Inconsistent statements cannot both be true together. At least one statement must be wrong, but which one that may be is an open question. Again, both statements may be wrong.

It would be inconsistent to say that the driver of a motor car was a white male, and later that he was a black male. Either description, but not both, may be accurate, or both may be wrong, as where the driver was a female.

Inconsistency damages evidence. It shows that something is wrong with it somewhere, but by itself, it does not show what that wrong is, or prove any facts. The harmful effect depends on where the inconsistency occurs, its nature, and how advocates deal with it.

Inconsistency may occur in direct evidence of the facts in issue, that is, the commission of the crime or the accused's identity as the offender; or inconsistency may arise in evidence of relevant facts or collateral facts.

Inconsistency in direct evidence about a fact such as the identification of the offender, if not explained, or shown to be due to a mistake, may be fatal to credibility. If an eye-witness who must know the facts gives inconsistent evidence, it may be concluded that he is lying, or at least that his evidence cannot be trusted.

Inconsistency about relevant facts (those from which a fact in issue may be inferred) may vary in its effect on credibility.

Details may be material in a chain of circumstantial evidence from which a main fact may be inferred. Variations may affect such inferences crucially, and arouse suspicions about lying.

Inconsistency in evidence of collateral facts (those affecting credibility or other subordinate facts) may be important. At times, even minute inconsistency may seem sinister.

But many trifling inconsistencies, such as those caused by the common fallibility of observation and memory of witnesses to the same event, have no significance for credibility. Magistrates should be aware of the tendency of advocates to exaggerate the effect of these discrepancies.

Where inconsistency occurs, there is also the question of whether it is found in the evidence of one only, or of two or more, witnesses, and whether they are called for the prosecution or the defence.

The term "inconsistency" here refers only to witnesses who support the same version of the facts. Usually witnesses who tell the same story are called by the same party. But there are exceptions; thus an accused's relative called reluctantly as a prosecution witness, may try to support the defence story.

Where witnesses try to tell the same story, regardless of who called them, inconsistency means that they have failed to do so, and is thus a defect which makes their evidence unreasonable.

This differs from the normal conflict between the prosecution and the defence versions of the facts. The term "contradiction" is preferred for this. Contradiction is neither a failure of evidence to achieve its aim, nor a defect, nor is it unreasonable. It simply obliges the court to choose between two versions of the facts.

Inconsistency in the evidence of a single witness is often more damaging than where the stories of two or more witnesses diverge. Unless a single witness can explain his inconsistency as a mistake or misunderstanding he may be discredited, especially if he must know the truth. But if two or more witnesses differ, any one of them may be accurate or inaccurate.

If serious inconsistency about material facts emerges in prosecution evidence, then because of the burden of proof and the standard of proof required for conviction, a reasonable doubt may be raised, leading to acquittal.

In defence evidence, material inconsistency may not be so critical since the defence needs prove nothing and needs only raise a reasonable doubt to succeed, for example, if inconsistent evidence leads a court to reject an alibi, this does not place the accused at the scene of the crime.

The effect of inconsistency in evidence also depends on how advocates deal with it. They try to repair damage caused by inconsistency in their own witnesses by correcting it, or by explaining it as a mistake rather than as the result of lying, which would be more harmful.

A cross-examiner will try to exploit any inconsistency found in his opponent's witnesses by showing that they are lying rather than mistaken, and by expanding the damage in order to discredit them as widely as possible.

Where no inconsistency has emerged in an opponent's evidence, a cross-examiner may try to create it by indirect tactics which lead one witness, or two or more, into conflicting statements. Again his aim will be to expose them as liars, not as mistaken.

Although cross-examiners usually seek in these direct ways to magnify the destructive effect of inconsistency on credibility, another approach is open to them. As soon as inconsistency emerges clearly in an opponent's evidence, cross-examination may be stopped. This prevents the witness from correcting the inconsistency, unless the opponent is able to eliminate or explain it satisfactorily in re-examination. Otherwise, it can be emphasized in the closing speech.

(c) Improbability

Evidence is unreasonable if the facts described are too improbable to be believed. This may either be the result of mistaken observation or memory, or it may be caused by lying.

What is probability? This question has vexed philosophers down the ages, and may be left to them. Attempts to answer it are simply verbal formulations which add nothing for practical purposes.

The facts alleged, singly, in combination, or which make up a whole story, may seem, or be made to seem, more or less likely to have happened. Usually, they concern human nature and conduct.

The only test of probability is practical judgment based on ordinary experience of life. No rules are possible about this quality of evidence as a guide to what evidence should be accepted or rejected. Unlike impossibility, conclusions based on improbability are never inevitable. It is difficult for advocates to present arguments about it, one way or another.

The typical questions of probability which arise in criminal trials are not usually statistical or mathematical, apart from some technical evidence such as fingerprint evidence or evidence about the frequency of blood groups in the population.

But the degree of probability always matters, although it cannot be expressed quantitatively. The term "improbable" denotes something which is unlikely to have happened. Improbable facts may range from those which are rather unlikely, yet possible and credible, to those which are so absurd as to be beyond belief.

In the course of a trial the question of whether evidence is improbable is likely to arise constantly. Even where it is not raised in evidence-in-chief, if there are any grounds for challenge, the issue will arise in cross-examination and in closing speeches.

Improbability and inconsistency are often found together, for example, inconsistency may arise from a dishonest witness's attempts to meet a challenge on the ground of improbability.

A cross-examiner may increase the degree of improbability by expanding the story in as much detail as possible, to the point of absurdity and rejection. He will draw out its unlikely implications and will show how it does not fit into the context of the reality shown by other acceptable evidence.

Magistrates may disbelieve evidence because it is too improbable, without necessarily deciding whether this is due to lying or mistake. But a cross-examiner will try, so far as he can, to show that lying is the explanation, since this is likely to damage the evidence to the widest extent.

The effect of mistaken evidence tends to be confined to the facts which are shown to be inaccurate for that reason. Other evidence may not be tainted by this, unless something wider is shown, such as the general unreliability of the witness's observation or memory, bias, or a tendency to exaggerate.

But if a cross-examiner can show that the improbability of evidence is the result of lying, this does apply more widely; it could discredit the witness and undermine any part of his evidence.

There are various pointers to these alternative causes for improbability.

A crucial test is the witness's knowledge of the facts; if he must know them, evidence which is rejected as too improbable may well be false.

Motivation may count. Improbable evidence given by motivated witnesses may seem more likely to be untruthful than mistaken. The extent of a witness's commitment to his evidence, ranging from half-hearted suggestion to dogmatic assertion, may suggest how involved he is personally. On the other hand, improbable evidence given by independent witnesses may appear more likely to be mistaken.

The existence of circumstances which could have led to mistaken observation or memory, would support the view that this explained the improbability. A witness who insists on his improbable testimony about something which he saw in ideal conditions of observation, may be more easily distrusted as a liar, than one who saw the incident from afar, in darkness, and who could thus be mistaken.

The nature and the degree of improbability, and when it became apparent, may be a guide to whether or not evidence is sincere. If the improbability of the evidence emerged only in the trial, a witness who gave it need not necessarily have been in bad faith. But if the story is really ridiculous it may seem that the witness must have known that, and that his story is false.

No general statement can be made about the type and degree of improbability which ought to lead to the rejection of evidence. Obviously, that facts are unusual is not a satisfactory ground for disbelieving them.

Every day, in criminal courts, witnesses testify truthfully about many things which might strike the average person as hard to believe. Today, as a result of the growth of the media, people tend to be less surprised about unusual varieties of behaviour than they were formerly. An open mind and some imagination are essential on the bench. Court experience helps to develop this. Due allowance must always be made for any socio-cultural differences in modes of thinking and conduct in various strata of society. Realism is indispensable. Magistrates, of course, being drawn from the community and still being part of it, have an advantage here.

The more the amount of evidence and variety of tests applied, the easier the decision becomes. After all the evidence has been weighed, any part of it which is held to be too improbable, may be rejected.

But however they decide the facts, magistrates should never lose sight of the requirement, by law, that any conviction must be based on proof of guilt beyond reasonable doubt, not on any degree of probability.

(d) Lack of realism

Used with care, an impression of the "realism" of evidence may contribute to a decision, without being a basis for it, by itself. Evidence may be compared with usual forms of truthful evidence. Real facts occur in a setting of other facts and personal reactions, which may colour reports, giving them the ring of truth.

False stories often focus anxiously on essentials, omitting any background which could make the event seem real — because it did not exist and has not been invented, as where an eyewitness to a dramatic event describes only the bare facts, without surrounding details or any natural personal response. Of course, some genuine testimony, from police witnesses, for instance, is typically flat, objective and neutral.

One-way and dogmatic evidence about an unclear event may be suspect. A true report might state doubts, odd facts, elements pointing both ways, and be incomplete because the witness does not know some material facts. But again, evidence may be one-way and firm, because it is accurate and the witness is sure.

These are tendencies, not rules. There is no substitute for good judgment.

2. Comparison of evidence

Two of the three tests of the credibility of evidence have been reviewed — whether the witness is trusted (Chapter 7); and whether evidence is reasonable. But even if evidence passes these two tests, this is not enough for belief in it. It is essential to apply the remaining test also, that is to assess that evidence in the context of all the other evidence.

A single witness may seem trustworthy and his story may seem reasonable. If so, this evidence is plausible. But is it true?

For a confident decision, a comparative approach is more reliable than judging one person and his story in isolation. The superior feature of a criminal trial is the comparison of evidence from several persons for support or contradiction about the same facts.

Also, by law, it is a court's duty to consider all the evidence and it would be improper to ignore any, whether it is accepted or not.

How evidence agrees with or contradicts other evidence will now be considered with regard to the main categories — direct (eyewitness) evidence of the facts in issue, for example, that the accused is the man who drove off in the stolen car, or evidence of relevant facts (circumstantial evidence) from which the facts in issue may be inferred, such as finding the car parked outside his flat and keys which fit it in his pocket. Similar principles apply to collateral evidence (relating to credibility or subordinate topics).

(a) Agreement of evidence

Whether the agreement of several witnesses about the facts in issue favours accuracy depends on the circumstances.

Where the witnesses are independent and unconnected, they would not be suspected of collusion in inventing a common story and their evidence is likely to seem truthful.

The more of such witnesses there are, the less probable it may seem that they are mistaken. They would all, separately, have had to make the same mistake. But this requires qualification.

A common factor can lead to a common mistake, even if there are many witnesses.

The subject of observation, could be the cause, for instance, it has been known for a number of honest witnesses to be mistaken in recognizing an accused as the offender, because of a strong resemblance between the people observed at the scene.

Another common factor is the effect of suggestion, even on unconnected witnesses. Examples include an unfair identification parade which leads all the witnesses to identify the wrong person; or media comment or discussion before giving evidence which influences all the witnesses into giving similar mistaken evidence.

If the evidence of several associated and motivated witnesses agrees about the facts in issue, care is needed. Their association gives them an opportunity of fabricating a story together. Their motives, if strong enough, will lead them to do so. As illustrations, in prosecution evidence, police witnesses could write up their notebooks together with some false twist, and in defence evidence, the accused and his family could make up an alibi.

Witnesses may also agree in their evidence about relevant facts (circumstantial evidence) from which facts in issue may be inferred. Their evidence may refer to the same facts. But it need not, and usually, does not, do so. It would be enough if it fitted together as a pattern. Agreement here is a question of meaningful consistency so that the evidence interlocks, rather than of identical evidence.

Such circumstantial evidence given by several witnesses may be illustrated in a charge of breaking a shop window and stealing cigarettes.

Witness 1 hears an alarm go off and sees a girl wearing a blue anorak running near the shop. Witness 2, a police officer, stops the accused several streets away; she is wearing a blue anorak, and has twenty packets of cigarettes in a plastic bag. Witness 3, the sergeant at the police station, sees that her hand is cut and bleeding. Witness 4, the shop manager, testifies that twenty packets of that brand of cigarettes were missing.

The evidence of the witnesses agrees in the sense of fitting together in a significant pattern, as a basis for an inference of guilt.

Witnesses who give circumstantial evidence, usually testify to different facts and are often unconnected and independent. If so, collusion is unlikely, and the evidence may be accepted as credible. This, of course, would only establish the relevant facts. The inference to be drawn from them is another matter.

For circumstantial evidence to be false, a deliberate plot would be necessary. This would require association between the witnesses, very strong motivation, and some imagination and skill. It might be easier to lie about the facts in issue directly. Where witnesses give consistent circumstantial evidence, a challenge to its credibility is uncommon, but not completely unknown.

In extreme instances, the defence may allege a police conspiracy to convict the accused by fabricating circumstantial evidence, for example by "planting" drugs to incriminate him, or by false attribution of admissions of guilt.

Unless it is supported by credible defence evidence, such a challenge usually faces great difficulties, including the need to show motives in police witnesses strong enough to make them incur the risks involved. Yet, at times, such criminal conduct by police has been proved.

If independent and unconnected witnesses give a consistent pattern of circumstantial evidence, to accuse them of lying may seem absurd. So, as a last resort, cross-examiners often suggest that they are mistaken. But this may be just as unreasonable. All the witnesses are unlikely to be mistaken about all the distinct facts unless some common cause can be shown.

In circumstantial evidence, the real issue is less likely to be whether a consistent chain of relevant facts is accurate, than the inference to be drawn from them.

The effect of agreement in direct or circumstantial evidence, may now be summed up.

If the evidence agrees to the point of being too uniform, whether this arises from accuracy or invention, always depends on circumstances. Generally, a consistent body of evidence pointing in the same direction, may have some weight, but must still be looked at critically.

Crucial tests are whether the witnesses are connected; whether they are motivated; and whether any common cause such as discussion could have led to mistaken evidence. If these sources of doubt are excluded, the effect of agreement of evidence will be greater.

(b) Contradiction of evidence

As has already been explained, "inconsistency" is an internal conflict of evidence within the prosecution case or within the defence case. By contrast "contradiction" is a conflict between the prosecution case and the defence case. It is the norm in our adversarial system. It is not a defect in either party's case. It obliges the court to choose between two versions of the facts.

When one set of witnesses contradicts the other, this creates a problem for the court, but it also contributes to the solution. Contradiction in evidence is of crucial importance in lie detection. It is superior to an evaluation of anything said by a single person, because testimonies can be compared.

In criminal trials, extracting the truth or detecting lies does not depend solely on the court's impression of a single witness or his evidence in isolation, although this may be a first approach.

As explained, a cross-examiner will challenge a lying witness with the aim of weakening or destroying two grounds for belief − trust in the witness, and the view that his evidence is reasonable. This rarely causes a witness to confess that he is lying. Destructive cross-examination may either have no impact, or, at best, it may weaken the evidence without destroying it.

An advocate should also put his contrary version of the facts to the witness so far as he knows them, but a liar will rarely concede them.

One typical result is that the cross-examiner cannot show any obvious grounds for distrusting the witness or for finding his evidence unreasonable; if so, the lying evidence survives cross-examination unscathed, and is then, at least plausible.

Even if grounds for distrusting the witness or for finding his evidence unreasonable emerge in cross-examination, they are rarely conclusive at that stage; the evidence may be greatly weakened, yet not destroyed. In these two situations, there may be no obvious reason to reject plausible or even doubtful evidence.

Here the value of contradiction of evidence can be seen. If the court forms trust in another witness, or witnesses, and finds their evidence reasonable, this may overcome the plausible or weakened lying evidence.

Contradiction of false by truthful evidence is a key to lie detection. Assessment of one part of the evidence helps assessment of another part.

This example is over-simplified. The evaluation of evidence is a comparative approach in which all parts of it are seen in a relationship of agreement or contradiction. This is what makes sound and confident decisions possible. Credibility is never self-evident. Good judgment, including lie detection, depends on this integrated approach whereby a trial becomes more than the sum of its parts.

Chapter 9

Opinion evidence

Generally, witnesses testify about facts which they perceived by means of their senses, not about inferences from these facts. If, after assessment in the ways discussed previously, evidence of perceived facts is found to be free from errors and lies, and to be reliable and credible, those facts are proved.

But at times witnesses may go further by drawing inferences from the perceived facts. These inferences may range from a lay witness's impressions, for example, that a pub was busy, to an expert witness's opinion, for example that brakes were faulty before they were damaged in an accident. Although opinions also state facts, they are derived from other facts which are perceived.

Decisions about the admissibility of opinion evidence are governed by the law of evidence about which magistrates may consult their clerks. The rules of evidence are not the subject of this book, but the general rule is that evidence of facts, but not of opinions, may be admitted. The principle is that a witness's opinion does not matter and that only the court may draw inferences from the facts, especially about the "ultimate issue" of guilt or innocence.

The main exception to the rule is that a suitably qualified expert may state his opinion on facts requiring his expertise – but only to give a court information about the facts beyond its knowledge, experience and capacity to decide. For this purpose, magistrates assess the suitability of the witness's qualifications, whether they are professional or informal.

1. Facts underlying opinions

In assessing expert evidence, questions of fact must be distinguished from questions of opinion.

The facts on which the opinion is based may be in dispute. It must be clear whether this factual information is accurate and complete before evaluating the opinion.

Sources of evidence may vary. An expert may describe what he saw as a lay witness, but not as an expert. He may describe facts, such as details of a blood analysis, which are accessible only to him as an expert. But he must have seen these facts himself and should not repeat hearsay evidence of tests.

A professional person may give expert information about facts to be proved by lay witnesses. But what the expert is told out of court, or a hypothesis put to him in court, is not evidence. Unless these facts are proved by lay witnesses, any opinion based on them is of no value.

Lay witnesses to facts underlying the expert's opinion would testify and be cross-examined constructively or destructively in the ordinary way.

The expert witness is likely to be cross-examined about pre-trial information given to him, and about any disputed facts which he perceived personally – whether or not they are within his field of expertise – usually on the ground that he is mistaken. A cross-examiner might also seek favourable evidence in the expert's observations.

Typically, a cross-examiner might ask an expert to agree that his opinion is based on certain facts; that they are disputed; that for all he knows they may be different; and that on the alternative facts his opinion might be different. The final thrust is to ask what his opinion would then be. This will expose the factual foundation for the opinion, and perhaps underlying weaknesses, but it may also raise another possibility. If that is a reasonable one, to resist this line of challenge could be adverse to the opinion.

2. Inferences from proved facts

Once facts are proved, the question is whether the correct inference has been drawn from them.

An expert's jargon may be an obstacle to clarity. Advocates, familiar with it, may not realize that terms or concepts are obscure. When opinions are put in plain language, many issues which seemed to be technical may become capable of decision by common sense.

Expert evidence is admitted to help magistrates decide the case, not to replace them. While an opinion should be considered carefully, it is not binding. This is obvious where it is obscure, or clashes with another opinion or lay evidence. But if expert evidence is clear and uncontradicted, there may be no good reason for not accepting it.

Expert witnesses are usually unconnected with the case. Their duty under the oath or affirmation may be reinforced by the ethics of their professions. Generally, their opinions are treated with respect, and, if challenged, are said to be mistaken or unreliable, not false.

But an expert witness is not an independent assessor appointed by the court to reach an impartial decision. He is in the arena with the adversaries, and is instructed and paid by one of them, perhaps regularly. If he advised the party who called him, he may be reluctant to depart from his advice, or from what he said in a report produced in court. It would be unrealistic and contrary to experience to deny that opinions may be biased, as this view states, "it is often quite surprising to see with what facility and to what extent, their views can be made to correspond with the wishes or the interests of the parties who call them" [Taylor, *Treatise on the Law of Evidence*, 12th edn at p 59].

Many expert witnesses are persons of integrity who would not willingly mis-state a simple fact. Yet, without realizing it, they may allow their opinions to be influenced in favour of the party who instructed them.

The factors in the situation which could lead to bias may be obvious to magistrates even without emphasis in cross-examination. Anyway, expert witnesses are unlikely to concede that they have been affected by their instructions.

In cross-examination, bias, partiality or unreasonable dogmatism may emerge more clearly when the focus is on the opinion and its relation to other evidence. Inconsistency or improbability in the opinion may be exposed, or it may be effectively contradicted by other lay or expert evidence. It may be seen that the opinion has been stated firmly where there should be some doubt, or with doubt where there should be firmness.

A cross-examiner may put an interpretation of undisputed facts to an expert which differs from his opinion. By suggesting subtle adjustments here and there, he may try to insinuate the inference which he desires.

An advocate must put his contentions to his opponent's witnesses who know the relevant facts, so that they can deny or comment on them. An expert who states an adverse opinion is likely to be confronted directly in cross-examination by a contradictory assertion. Unless this is done, whether in detail or in one comprehensive question, magistrates may form the view that the unchallenged adverse opinion has been accepted.

A question often put to an expert is whether his findings are "consistent" with some fact in the case, for example, whether an incised wound was consistent with being caused by a sharp instrument, followed by asking whether this consistency applies to a knife exhibited.

If this consistency is accepted, by itself, and if there are no special features to link that wound with that knife, it is simply an inconclusive item of circumstantial evidence. It means that these two facts, the wound and the knife, could have co-existed when the blow was struck, although the opinion does not prove that this knife caused the wound – any sharp instrument might have done so. But, depending on the context, such an opinion could be important, for example to exclude an alleged punch as the cause.

Sometimes advocates try to extend expert opinion beyond proper limits, for example by asking if a wound is consistent with an account of the attack. The opinion may be relevant to how the blow was struck, but not to who struck it or why. The wound may be "consistent" with the whole event, by not excluding its possibility. An opinion applied to unconnected and remote facts may cease to be evidence at all.

The proposed misuse of opinion evidence is not un-common. The aim is to use an expert's status to support a story about the facts in issue, to which it does not refer. It is often due to a lack of lay evidence about the event.

An expert's opinion should not be evaluated in isolation. Like any evidence it must be assessed in the context of the whole of the evidence in the trial. Magistrates may then prefer lay evidence of perceived facts, to expert opinion.

To illustrate this, in a trial for a drink and driving offence, an expert's opinion may be that alcohol in an accused's blood was due to drinking before his driving ceased. But if the accused's testimony that it was due to drinking after he stopped driving is accepted, or raises a reasonable doubt, he must be acquitted.

If the opinions of two experts clash, and are irreconcilable, they cannot both be right. The conflicting opinions may then neutralize each other, the court deciding that it cannot accept either as reliable.

Alternatively, magistrates may prefer one opinion to the other, after evaluating each one on its merits in relation to the whole of the evidence.

Very technical evidence may be difficult to assess. The more specialized it is, the more important expert opinion may become, although no evidence should ever be accepted uncritically. If highly qualified experts state conflicting opinions, their comparative status and authority may count, thus a distinguished consultant surgeon's opinion about a medical condition might overcome the contrary view of a newly-qualified general practitioner.

Expert witnesses can state opinions in the fields of their expertise only, and not on other subjects. Opinions which stray beyond this are inadmissible, or, in marginal circumstances, of doubtful value. Thus, by various techniques, a cross-examiner may try to show that an opinion or part of it, is inadmissible.

One method is to build up, with the expert's off-guard co-operation, an impressive picture of his specialized knowledge and experience, excluding what relates directly to the issue.

A witness who claims expertise in a relevant field may be asked if he had experience of identical facts; if he claims this too, a cross-examiner may probe for meaningful differences between that experience and the present issues.

One way in which expert evidence may become distorted is where advocates edit it against the witness's wishes. This can happen either in examination-in-chief or in cross-examination.

Expert witnesses may be inhibited by tightly controlled patterns of questioning which prevent them from answering some questions fully, or from covering other significant points about which no questions are asked at all.

Where it seems possible that this has happened the opponent ought to ensure that the omitted evidence is brought out.

In evaluating opinion evidence, magistrates should take account of adversarial tactics which are designed to affect their judgment.

Chapter 10

Circumstantial evidence

In criminal trials, most facts are proved by oral testimony, and it is in this context that documents or exhibits become admissible, relevant, and meaningful, although partly they speak for themselves.

Direct evidence is a report of a fact in issue, a relevant fact, or a collateral fact, which a witness perceived personally using his senses.

It excludes anything perceived by another person (hearsay) or an opinion about facts, since that goes beyond what was perceived. If direct evidence of any fact is accepted as truthful and accurate, it is proved.

Facts in issue are those which the prosecution must prove for conviction, that is, the commission of the crime with the necessary intention, and the identity of the accused as the offender. Other facts in issue are those, apart from a mere denial of the prosecution case, which would establish a defence if proved.

Relevant facts are those from which the existence or non-existence of a fact in issue may be inferred.

Collateral facts are those affecting the credibility of a witness or other subordinate facts, such as evidence about how a confession was obtained if its admissibility is in dispute.

Circumstantial evidence, as distinct from direct evidence, is evidence of relevant facts – those from which the existence or non-existence of a fact in issue may be inferred.

Direct evidence of the facts in issue is often unavailable.

Many crimes occur when no one is watching, or in darkness. They may be unseen or the offender may not be identifiable.

The prosecution must often rely on proving part of the case by means of an incriminating inference about the facts in issue, drawn from circumstantial evidence. This may be combined with direct evidence of the facts in issue.

The validity of a conviction based on circumstantial evidence depends on proof of the relevant facts, and on drawing the correct inference from them.

All the evidence in the trial should be taken into account in deciding whether or not to accept the evidence of relevant facts and, if they are proved, what inference to draw.

Even if the relevant facts are beyond doubt, direct evidence may contradict an inference.

If shoes with a unique defect, worn by an accused, undoubtedly match footprints in soil under a window through which a burglar entered a house, magistrates may be asked to infer that the accused was the intruder. But if the accused claims that he bought the shoes in a market after the burglary, this contradicts the inference linking him to the crime. Even the certainty that the offender wore those shoes does not destroy the accused's story.

1. Forms of circumstantial evidence

The value of circumstantial evidence depends on the common connections between facts. A criminal event occurs in reality, not in isolation. Facts cannot be inconsistent and are often inter-related even if only remotely. Hence a central fact may be inferred from minor facts which, by themselves, mean little or nothing.

Circumstantial evidence may take many forms. To classify is pointless but it is helpful to divide relevant facts into those which happened before, during and after the event in issue. It is also noteworthy that human nature and conduct are the usual subjects of the evidence.

Evidence is often admitted to show that the accused had a motive for committing the crime, to increase the probability that he did commit it. It may refer to statements of intention such as threats, or acts or situations from which a motive may be inferred.

Acts which suggest that the crime was being planned or prepared, could point to guilt, as where an accused is seen with a weapon, or some object which the offender may have used.

Such evidence may support the prosecution case, but it may not suffice to link an accused with the crime, for example, he may have given up his original intention. Yet an absence of evidence of motive, planning of or preparation for the crime may not help the defence. Many serious crimes are committed without forethought or for trivial reasons.

Evidence of facts which are close in time and place to the commission of a crime, is generally admissible, and could set up a network of surrounding facts from which the facts in issue may be inferred. It may be difficult to separate such circumstantial evidence from direct evidence of the facts in issue.

If direct eyewitness identification of the accused as the offender is accepted, this would be proved. But his implication is usually a hotly contested issue, as where Crown witnesses are challenged as mistaken, and the defence is an alibi. If so, the prosecution may seek support from circumstantial evidence.

The prosecution may lead circumstantial evidence to show that an accused had the opportunity to commit the crime, for example, that he was seen at or near the scene around that time, or that he lived nearby or had a motor cycle.

Circumstantial evidence of various facts which follow the commission of a crime, may be significant.

Forensic evidence is an important category of post-event circumstantial evidence. An offender may leave personal traces at a scene or on a victim, or may carry away on his person traces from the scene or the victim. An accused's injuries may link him to a violent incident or a traffic accident.

Real evidence linked with both the crime and accused may be incriminating, for example articles produced as exhibits (such as a knife or crowbar) which were found in his possession and which could have been used in the crime.

Evidence of possession, in suspicious circumstances, of recently stolen goods is a common type of circumstantial evidence. The possibility of an adverse inference may be met if this is explained in a way which is consistent with innocence. Either no explanation or an incredible one may be equally ineffective for the defence.

Questions sometimes arise about the identification of the property; unless it is properly identified as the stolen property, this evidence would be pointless.

It could be adverse to the accused if evidence were led to prove conduct on his part aimed at avoiding conviction. Some such evidence, for example that he ran away from the police, or that, although he now has a large beard, he did not have it around the date of the crime, might be admissible, the inference being that he has tried to impede recognition.

But other evidence of the accused's conduct after the time of the crime could raise questions of admissibility if the prosecutor sought to lead it, since it may impute other crimes, attack character, or be prejudicial. Examples include concealing, destroying, interfering with, or fabricating real evidence, or intimidating witnesses.

A wide spectrum of circumstantial evidence refers to things said or not said by an accused, which could have harmful implications. On a common sense basis, if he refuses or fails to explain some incriminating situation, or explains it in an incredible or false way, or does not explain it at the earliest stage, particularly when it could have been confirmed, this may suggest a guilty state of mind.

But statements by the accused, or failure to make a statement, cannot be considered on a common sense basis alone. There are legal limits to the admissibility of such evidence or the propriety of drawing such adverse inferences.

Questions of the admissibility of evidence of a statement made by the accused may depend on whether he was a suspect or had been cautioned, or had made the statement voluntarily or under circumstances of oppression.

Questions about the propriety of drawing adverse inferences from something which the accused did not say may depend on whether his right to silence was operative at the time. If it was, no comment should be made on it.

An accused's confession to the police, if proved by admissible evidence, and especially if it refers to facts which only the offender would know, might be conclusive. But often an accused will deny making such a statement or indeed any statement, to the police.

So circumstantial evidence of what an accused did or did not say after the time of a crime, and drawing inferences from this, is only appropriate in certain situations.

2. Defence challenge to circumstantial evidence

Circumstantial evidence is usually led for the prosecution, not the defence. The defence may challenge it in various ways.

The defence may lead direct evidence about the facts in issue, to contradict an incriminating inference from the circumstantial evidence, for example, the accused may testify that he was not at the scene, or that no crime was committed.

The defence may also cross-examine witnesses who give circumstantial evidence.

The most radical approach is to undermine the inference by attacking the individual facts on which an inference is based. But it may seem unreasonable, where the witnesses are independent and are not associated, to suggest that all or some of them are mistaken about simple facts, or are part of a lying conspiracy to convict the accused. Yet it may be helpful to ask if they have discussed their evidence.

An argument presented to the court − not to witnesses − is the remaining defence tactic. Here it may challenge the inference from the facts, and emphasize the way in which it is contradicted by the defence's own direct evidence.

3. Probative value of circumstantial evidence

Proof of guilt by circumstantial evidence may be as strong as, or stronger than, proof by eyewitness evidence. It may be even more convincing if circumstantial evidence and direct evidence are combined.

Generally, only one fact in issue − either the commission of the crime or the identity of the accused as the offender − will depend on this form of proof, the other fact in issue being undisputed.

Each relevant fact must first be proved separately, by direct evidence, independently of any inference which may follow from it. The inference cannot in any way support the proof of the facts on which it depends.

An inference from circumstantial evidence is strengthened by the number and variety of relevant facts on which it is based. Such an inference can never be a matter of absolute logic as in mathematics. But it is a universal and essential part of everyday thinking, whereby a meaning arises in the mind spontaneously which explains the separate facts.

Probability, ranging from a minimal to an overwhelming degree, enters into such inferences. Yet, although the highest degree of probability is obviously essential to conviction, that is not the test. The standard for proof of guilt is a psychological one, a state of mind and feeling; the tribunal must be satisfied beyond reasonable doubt. Unless this test is met, the accused must be acquitted, however likely it may be that he is guilty.

But this test will be applied to the whole mass of the oral, documentary and real evidence presented by both parties, not simply to a single inference from circumstantial evidence. It is the concurrence and contradiction of all the evidence, considered together, which may be persuasive.

For conviction, the inference from the relevant facts must do more than explain them reasonably. Conviction should follow only if the facts and the inference meet the standard of proof required for a criminal conviction.

Chapter 11

Witnesses

Some typical problems concerning witnesses are selected for comment in this chapter. They can be discussed only in general terms and this must be seen for what it is — as guidance, but not as rules to be followed. An emphatic warning against pre-judgment is necessary. The comments which follow refer to tendencies. It is an overriding principle that the facts of each trial are unique and that all evidence must be assessed on its merits in the given situation. Yet, because of the frequency and similarity of many such problems, to discuss them in general terms can be helpful.

1. Prosecution witnesses

Usually, prosecution evidence is given by the complainant, eyewitnesses, circumstantial witnesses, and police witnesses.

A crucial question, which applies to all prosecution witnesses, is whether they are motivated or independent.

Apart from this, each category presents typical problems.

(a) Complainants

Complainants are presented as the victims of crimes but they have no special status as witnesses; the accuracy of their evidence is an open question like any other.

A complainant may be an eyewitness, such as a shopkeeper who saw a theft in his shop. Again a complainant may just be a circumstantial witness, as in the case of a householder who finds a window open.

A complainant's testimony may be objective and uncontested, so that it is accepted without difficulty, for example when it relates to finding that a car was stolen.

A complainant may be mistaken or unreliable, for example, in identifying a burglar seen running from his garden.

A complainant may lie. For gain, or from malice, he may invent or exaggerate a crime, or he may attribute a genuine crime to an innocent accused. In a burglary charge, a householder may add falsely to the list of stolen goods to inflate an insurance claim. Where self-defence is the plea, the alleged victim may actually have been the aggressor.

Child complainants, in indecency charges, for instance, raise special problems. Questions of law about their competency as witnesses, corroboration or warnings, are not discussed here. Changes in rules and procedures are under consideration.

A major problem is to minimize stress for the child arising from the court situation, the accused's presence, and the sensitive nature of the evidence.

The prosecutor's problem may be to elicit any evidence at all from an inarticulate child. The prohibition of leading on matters in issue is sometimes relaxed.

The defence problem may be to challenge the evidence without upsetting the child or antagonizing the bench.

Magistrates may have difficulty in assessing a child's evidence in this context. They should not, of course, fill in the gaps by speculation.

Psychology is full of controversies about the reliability and credibility of child evidence, and no general statement may be made about it. Child witnesses differ, as do adults, and in any event the court assesses the particular child witness, not children in general.

(b) Eyewitnesses

Eyewitness evidence, if accepted, proves the facts in issue directly. Whether the witness is independent or motivated can be vital.

The evidence of an independent witness may have substantial weight, as in a careless driving charge, where a pedestrian describes how motor cars came to collide.

But the defence may challenge independent and sincere eyewitness evidence as mistaken or unreliable. Visual identification is one of the most vulnerable types. So too, is evidence of something obscure or ambiguous, such as suspicious conduct in a car park.

Independent witnesses may believe that they are being sincere, yet their evidence may be biased, for instance an old person who saw the accident may be prejudiced against young "tearaway" drivers of the accused's age group − or a mother may be sympathetic to such a person.

Outright lying in eyewitness evidence usually constitutes perjury, and is only to be expected in strongly motivated witnesses.

Accomplices called by the prosecution as eyewitnesses are often regarded as dubious because of their poor character and their motives for co-operating. Motives may include immunity from prosecution, or a lighter sentence if already convicted of the offence.

Accomplices may of course incriminate the accused without being eyewitnesses to the offence, as where they give evidence of receiving stolen goods from him.

Assessing the evidence of accomplices generally requires great care and is subject to legal requirements which should be known.

(c) Circumstantial witnesses

Prosecution witnesses to secondary facts from which the main facts may be inferred are often accepted as accurate. Each witness may testify to some minor fact which is significant only when several such facts are put together, so that guilt may be inferred from them. Of course once the relevant facts are proved, whether such an inference is justified is a question of judgment, not of evidence.

Some conditions may favour the accuracy of such evidence, as when the facts are often simple (for instance, that a man wore a red anorak), so that mistakes are unlikely.

Again, unconnected witnesses would have had no chance of influencing each other by discussion.

If they were independent, they would have no apparent motives for lying.

For these reasons, circumstantial evidence often has greater force than direct evidence. While it may not be difficult for a witness to lie about the main facts which he observed, circumstantial evidence may present an impressive network of facts which is unlikely to proceed from either mistake or falsehood. It may be unlikely that by mere chance a group of unconnected persons should each have observed a number of facts which fit together with a compelling effect so as to convey a definite meaning which explains them all.

Yet the defence sometimes contends that motivated witnesses, who are associated with each other, have conspired to fabricate circumstantial evidence.

Generally, it is the police who are the targets for such accusations, and, on occasion this accusation has proved to be true.

(d) Police witnesses

Since police witnesses testify in most trials, they merit fairly full consideration.

The police have no special status as witnesses, despite their role in enforcing criminal justice. Their evidence may be anything from a formality, for example, that a sample was delivered to a laboratory; to crucial testimony, for example that the accused made a full confession.

Police witnesses, like others, may be challenged as mistaken or untruthful. Attacks on police credibility ought to be responsible and based on information. Unless such attacks are supported by evidence from the accused or defence witnesses, they may be weak and open to criticism. If the defence attacks the character of a police witness, an attack on the accused's character may become admissible. The complex rules of evidence should be consulted on this.

Are police witnesses superior as observers? There is no reason to think that they have better natural faculties than other persons, although, for entry to the police force, they are likely to have good eyesight and hearing.

But the motivation and experience of police officers, and the possibility that they may have to testify about what they observe, may sharpen their attention to many facts.

There is no ground to suppose that the police have better natural memories than lay witnesses, but their recall of facts may be enhanced in ways which apply to them particularly. Because of the motivation and experience referred to above, which lead them to pay close attention to facts, a strong and clear image of facts may be formed, which resists forgetting and suggestion. This image is likely to be reinforced by the witness's further and continued involvement in the case which constantly refreshes his memory.

In carrying out their duties, and knowing that they may have to testify, it is routine for police officers to enter their observations in their notebooks or in reports, as soon as possible. Later, reference to these records will refresh their memories. Indeed in court, they are often allowed to do this from notes made at the time. Also, they often have to discuss their enquiries with colleagues, which again reminds them of their evidence.

Police officers – who are "professional witnesses" in a sense – may make a good impression, being of good appearance, smartly dressed, and having a confident bearing and way of testifying.

Although they should not argue a case, they have a basic grasp of criminal law, procedure and the rules of evidence. They gain experience as witnesses, especially in coping with cross-examination with self-control and restraint, even when their integrity is attacked.

For these reasons, where police witnesses are regarded as sincere, not surprisingly, their evidence is often accepted as accurate.

But there are also some unfavourable aspects of police evidence which may sometimes suggest that it is mistaken or unreliable.

Police witnesses may influence each other unintentionally. Often, they work in pairs or in teams. They must discuss their enquiries, note their observations, complete written reports, take witness statements, and communicate information to each other. They may consult criminal intelligence records which could be based on hearsay or speculation.

An accused's previous convictions may colour a witness's views.

The risk is that any of these activities may affect evidence by suggestion. This risk may be minimal in regard to facts which are recalled clearly and firmly, for example, that a child was injured in a road accident. But the risk may be great in regard to facts which are vague, obscure or ambiguous, for example in evidence of visual identification, or about the participation of individuals in a public disturbance.

A careful scrutiny of such evidence is required, and account should be taken of the possible effects of suggestion. Even if the police evidence is not shown to be mistaken, it may be rejected because of the possible element of unreliability, having regard to the prosecutor's obligation to prove guilt beyond reasonable doubt.

The possibility that police witnesses are biased must also be kept in mind. They must comply with their oath, like any witnesses. Moreover they should perform their duties fairly and impartially. But many witnesses fail to realize that their testimony is biased in one direction or another.

Common sources of bias in police evidence may be helpful qualities in other police duties. These sources include opposition to crime; alertness to and suspicion of wrong-doing; scepticism; determination to bring offenders to justice; the wish to be efficient; and the hope that guilty persons will be convicted.

The effect of bias in police evidence varies according to its strength and location.

It need not make the evidence inaccurate. Bias may simply lead to dogmatism or exaggeration of something which is a fact, and will be proved anyway. But bias in police evidence would be serious if it is so strong as to taint the evidence with real partisanship.

Biased police evidence may be suspect if it refers to inherently uncertain facts in issue, such as identity; the intangible elements in a crime; or vague, ambiguous or obscure facts of any kind.

Because of the heavy burden of proof on the prosecution, such police evidence might be rejected as mistaken or unreliable.

A cross-examiner may challenge a police witness openly and directly by contending that his evidence is biased and therefore inaccurate, but he should not expect this to be conceded. Instead it may be more effective to lead the witness, indirectly, to display his bias and dogmatism by the way in which he testifies.

One risk is that biased police views may affect the evidence of lay witnesses with whom they have been in contact during their enquiries, in taking witness statements, for instance.

Vulnerable areas include pre-trial procedures for identification of suspects, including taking descriptions, arranging confrontations, showing photographs, and the conduct of identification parades.

(e) Confessions

Police witnesses often testify to full confessions or partial admissions made to them by the accused. Since conviction will follow from accepting that evidence it is usually challenged on one of three grounds.

First, that the evidence is inadmissible by law, especially under statute and codes of practice. This involves questions of oppression, unreliability, or unfairness; the burden of proving or disproving the allegation; the standard of proof; and the trial within a trial procedure. Questions of admissibility of evidence are not within the plan of this book.

The second ground for challenge is that the evidence is or may be mistaken. Evidence of a confession is less likely to be mistaken where two officers heard it in the controlled circumstances of a police station; one wrote it down, read it over to the accused, and the accused and both officers signed it.

If evidence of a confession in such conditions is mistaken, both police officers would have made the same mistake at the same time, or in their recollections in court. How likely is it that they would both err in recalling a non-existent statement, or in reporting a statement in identically incorrect terms?

Full confessions are usually taken by officers in this way, but even if the conditions fell below this level, for example if the accused did not sign the statement, mistake can usually be ruled out. Here, if the evidence of the confession is indeed inaccurate, the explanation must be that the police witnesses are lying.

Partial admissions tending to incriminate are often made before suspects are detained in a police station, spontaneously in the course of enquiries at the scene of the crime or in the accused's home, for example.

Here, there is a greater chance of a mistake, for example, the statement might be misheard because of background noise; and its meaning may depend on tone of voice, and what was said before and afterwards. But again, if two officers describe firmly the same mistaken statement, simultaneous error on the part of each of them would have occurred.

If the accused was cautioned and charged, his answers will be written in one officer's notebook. This too is adverse to a contention that the reported statement is mistaken. Even if it was incorrectly noted, errors of memory are excluded if the notebook is in court.

Why then does the defence so often suggest that such evidence is mistaken rather than untruthful?

There can be a number of reasons. The defence may hope to avoid antagonizing the witnesses and to secure their co-operation — usually in vain.

The defence may wish to avoid making a poor impression on the court by an unreasonable suggestion that police witnesses are lying. If so, they often make matters worse.

To contend that police witnesses to a confession are mistaken, where they could only be lying, is obviously not genuine. The effect is one of insincerity, and a lack of confidence in the challenge. Moreover this misleads the court by directing its attention to the wrong factors for assessing the evidence. All this may damage or destroy the defence by showing its weakness.

Third, the defence may challenge the confession evidence as untruthful. The standards of police integrity in Great Britain are high. But police witnesses do, of course, lie at times, and have even been known to enter into a criminal conspiracy to convict innocent persons. Such miscarriages of justice cause great public concern, but they are exceptional. It would be unrealistic to see this as common or typical just as it would be to claim that all police evidence is truthful. Every attack on police credibility must be weighed on its own merits with an open mind.

When police evidence of confessions is attacked as untruthful, certain obstacles are common.

These include the suspect motivation, and perhaps the poor character, of the accused; expectations of how officers should behave; the grave consequences for those who commit perjury; and usually a lack of evidence that the police have a motive for lying.

Where malice may be the motive, the defence may refrain from claiming this as it may expose the accused's previous contacts with the police witness, and, hence, his previous convictions.

But sometimes the defence tries to prove malice by evidence of the accused's maltreatment by the police. The defence may, of course, always suggest that police witnesses have misconceived their role in the administration of justice, by seeking convictions at all costs — even by perjury.

Attacks on the credibility of police evidence of confessions lose impact unless the accused gives supporting evidence. If he does this, the credibility of the conflicting versions must be compared. Two questions which arise — "why should the accused confess?", and "why should a confession be retracted?" — will be discussed in regard to the accused as a witness; see page 114.

2. Defence witnesses

Defence evidence may be given by the accused, alone, or with the support of eyewitnesses, circumstantial witnesses, or alibi witnesses.

(a) The accused

It is never said in court, and is said here only to exclude it, that most trials end in a conviction. Statistically, where an accused denies his guilt, the odds are against his being truthful. But it would be absolutely improper, and entirely unjudicial, to take this into account to the slightest degree whatever. Any conviction where this occurred would be automatically quashed on appeal.

As explained in Chapter 2, an accused who denies the crime, must usually place himself at the scene of the crime to do so. Thus, he eliminates the question of his identification, wholly or partly.

But if he denies that he was present at the scene of the crime when it happened, whether or not he pleads alibi, he cannot then, personally, contest the crime.

The assessment of an accused's evidence should, as soon as possible, focus on whether he denies the crime, or his implication in it.

In assessing the accused's evidence, the question of his motivation is often unhelpful. He would aim at acquittal, whether he is innocent or guilty.

The impression made by an accused's evidence usually depends greatly on how he or she withstands cross-examination — the essential and crucial confrontation of parties, at the heart of a criminal trial.

If an accused emerges from cross-examination with flying colours, this may go far towards an acquittal. But if under cross-examination his evidence shows, or develops, inconsistencies, improbabilities, or confusion, the defence may be seriously damaged.

Rules of evidence, and their exceptions, protect an accused from attacks on his character, or reference to his previous conduct. A major principle is his right to remain silent from the time of his contacts with the police to the trial, where he can refrain from giving evidence, without comment on this.

In discussing the credibility of police evidence of confessions, two questions arose. The first was "why should the accused confess?" Offenders rarely commit crimes with the intention that afterwards they will surrender themselves to the police.

An offender, formerly of good character, may confess to an offence when he genuinely regrets the consequences, as in the case of a child killed by drunken driving. But this hardly applies to making a confession, denying it, and then pleading not guilty. Confessions due to remorse are rarely met in court.

An accused might confess as a result of police pressure or inducement. But since the confession was not made freely and voluntarily, evidence of it would be inadmissible.

The most usual reason for confessing is quite different, and is readily understandable. It is that the proof of guilt seems to be inevitable. The accused may be caught red-handed in the course of committing the crime, or there might be overwhelming eyewitness or circumstantial evidence to incriminate him.

If this is so, by confessing, a guilty accused has nothing to lose and may think that he has something to gain, such as bail, or a shorter sentence.

For such reasons, he may co-operate by incriminating an accomplice against whom he will testify in a trial, or he might disclose the location of stolen property. If he goes so far, he might not retract his confession later.

This offers an opening for defence cross-examination by asking the police witnesses what evidence there was against the accused when he confessed. If there was little or none, the confession might seem to be surprising. This may support the contention that the confession was obtained improperly, or that the evidence of a confession is false.

But if there was other strong incriminating evidence, this could explain the confession and there would be less need for police to lie unlawfully about a confession to secure the conviction. This may tend to support its truth.

Where an alleged confession is the only evidence against an accused, the evidence should be scrutinized with care. Unless his reason for confessing is explained, doubt may arise from this and the lack of supporting evidence.

If a guilty accused did confess, why would he retract his confession later, and plead not guilty? The answer is obvious. Perhaps refreshed after an ordeal, with time to think, and to discuss the matter with his associates and his lawyer, he may have thought up a possible defence, even though it is weak. If so, he must deny any confession which he made, and attack evidence of it as mistaken or untruthful.

(b) Eyewitnesses

If the accused in his evidence denies that he was at the scene of the crime, whether or not he pleads alibi, the defence is unlikely to call eyewitnesses to the crime; it is sufficient for acquittal that the accused was not there, or that there is reasonable doubt about this.

It is likely that the defence will call eyewitnesses only where the accused admits his presence at the scene, in which case two possible issues could arise.

The defence could be that the crime was not committed, or that, if it was committed, the accused was not involved in it.

The first issue is a question of observation of what persons did; even the second issue, the accused's involvement, is more a matter of relating actions to a person, than of visual identification.

As in eyewitness evidence for the prosecution, independent witnesses such as customers who just happened to be in a public house, or people who passed by in the street, may have more weight here than the accused's associates.

If defence eyewitnesses are called, prosecutors usually cross-examine independent eyewitnesses as mistaken and associates of the accused as lying.

(c) Circumstantial witnesses

The defence call circumstantial evidence less often than the prosecution do, but the same principles apply.

(d) Alibi witnesses

An alibi means a defence that the accused was elsewhere when the crime was committed.

A defence of alibi is appropriate to a crime which occurred at a fairly definite time and place only, not one which endured over a period, such as abstracting or diverting electricity.

The prosecutor is likely to cross-examine independent witnesses who support an alibi as to possible misidentification of the accused, or mistake about the time and place of the alibi.

The prosecutor is likely to cross-examine the accused's associates who support his alibi, as lying.

Whether alibi evidence is challenged as mistaken or untruthful, much may depend on the cross-examiner's skill. If the challenge meets with some success, the most likely result is to cast doubt on the alibi, not to demolish it completely at that stage. It may be so weakened that it is overcome by prosecution evidence to the effect that the accused was the offender.

Even if an alibi is destroyed, this may not prove any facts. Failure to prove that the accused was in Brighton at the material time, does not place him in Dover where the crime was committed, although it removes a barrier to such proof. A false alibi may have been invented to replace or support a genuine defence.

To break down false alibi evidence, a cross-examiner may have to explore minute details of the story − not for themselves, but to test credibility. Some witnesses may be found to have an excellent "memory" for some details, and an "amnesia" for others which create a difficulty for them.

A type of false alibi which is difficult to discredit is one which is accurate in all respects except the date and time. Sometimes, witnesses stage such an incident after the crime.

But the assessment of alibi evidence is not confined to that testimony. It must be considered in relation to contradictory evidence, and the evidence as a whole.

Chapter 12

The finding

So far, the principles of fact-finding have been set out systematically. In reaching a final decision, these principles are integrated and applied to actual problems. In this chapter, the essential matters for consideration at the stage of decision are focused, by reviewing earlier topics together in a condensed form.

1. No premature conclusions

While evidence is being given, magistrates naturally form impressions of witnesses and of the accuracy or inaccuracy of their testimony, such as a witness's apparent confusion under cross-examination about some fact. But although this process of registering and assimilating evidence, with some running assessment, is inevitable, no conclusions should be reached then. At this stage, both the law and common sense require suspension of judgment.

To reach any final judgment about part of the evidence, before hearing all of it, means that the remaining evidence will be ignored. It will count for nothing since a decision has already been reached. Likewise, closing speeches of advocates might just as well not be made.

It is the duty of a court to consider all the evidence called before it, as well as the addresses of advocates. To do otherwise and to decide issues prematurely, would contravene this fundamental judicial obligation.

It is also a matter of common sense that to jump to conclusions prematurely is unsound. Later evidence often contradicts earlier evidence, and may lead to a quite different view.

All evidence should be attended to with an open mind. There should be no prejudices, pre-judgments or stereotyped ideas, such as "is the accused yet another long-haired hooligan with earrings?" An open mind is quite compatible with weighing the evidence critically as it proceeds. But flexibility is crucial. Nothing should be decided at this stage.

Evidence often starts with scattered and isolated facts, which seem to have no meaning (unless it was brought out in an opening speech). It may be that insufficient thought was given to presentation. The bench will try to make sense of the evidence, and to grasp the situation as soon as possible. This is how a party's case becomes meaningful and is remembered.

The prosecution has an advantage because it calls its evidence first. It will usually add up to some coherent story, assisted by the statement of the crime which is charged.

But usually the defence, in cross-examination, will try to destroy, or at least raise doubts about, that story. it should also put its own case – a contradictory version of the facts – to the prosecution witnesses. Later, this is often supported by the evidence of the accused, and perhaps other defence witnesses. So conflicting accounts are heard all the time.

Although judgments should not be reached prematurely nobody's mind can work like a computer which registers all the data and gives the solution on the final press of a button. The normal psychological process consists of the continuous formation and dissolution of images in response to the evidence being heard.

A witness describes facts in some way, accurately or not. To be understood, his mere description creates an imagined picture.

But another account may be different. Earlier images may be corrected, merged with later ones, or one image

119

may replace another entirely. Yet any image of the facts should be provisional until the time for judgment.

Obviously, therefore, rigidity of mind is fatal to this process of adjusting images, and prevents proper consideration of evidence. A magistrate need not doubt his judgment because he keeps changing his mind in the course of the evidence. This flexibility of mind will eventually lead to a firm and sound decision — everything having been considered fully and fairly. The time for finality is when all the evidence has been heard, usually after the bench has retired to consider its finding.

2. Closing speeches

The content of a closing speech is a matter for the advocate, but it may determine the issues for final consideration. A well-constructed speech can be an agenda for judgment. It may settle facts when an advocate concedes any which are adverse to his case but which he cannot dispute.

In a well-prepared case, a defence advocate will draft his closing speech provisionally, before the trial starts, as a guide to the conduct of his case. All the evidence which he calls, and his cross-examinations, should lead up to this final argument. Naturally it must be open to adjustment in the light of what actually occurs. But the closing speech generally gives a case its structure. It is also an advocate's last tactical communication with the bench.

Magistrates should scan the closing speech for the issues to be decided, under reference to supporting or contradictory evidence. It may not impress by stressing strong points only while avoiding criticisms or weaknesses. Each case should be seen as a connected story.

3. Questions of law

Some questions of law which arise in the course of the evidence, are settled before the stage of considering the finding. These include the competence and compellability of witnesses, and objections to the admissibility of evidence. The bench need not consider them further, although, of course, these decisions may be appealed.

Where magistrates reject a defence submission that there is no case to answer because of a lack of evidence to prove an essential element in the prosecution case, this question will not arise again in considering the verdict.

Another type of "no case" submission may be that the prosecution evidence has been so discredited by cross-examination or is so manifestly unreliable that no reasonable tribunal could safely convict on it. Unless this is upheld by dismissal of every charge, the trial will go on. Whether or not defence evidence is then led, magistrates may still acquit, by applying the different test of whether or not guilt has been proved beyond reasonable doubt.

So, while this issue raised initially as a "no case" submission of mixed fact and law is still live at the finding stage, it now requires a final decision about the facts.

The main questions of law which arise in considering the finding include the application of the criminal law to the facts proved, in respect of acts done, states of mind, or the implication of the accused. This determines the questions of whether or not the crime charged was committed, and committed by the accused.

The other main group of questions involved in the finding are the requirements for proof of guilt, including corroboration or warnings in the form of self-direction where applicable, and in regard to the burden and standard of proof.

4. Facts in issue

In every trial, the facts in issue are (1) whether the crime charged was committed; and (2) whether the accused is the person who committed it. For conviction, the prosecutor must prove both.

As was explained in Chapter 2, by law, the defence need not concede anything in the prosecution case, but in practice it usually admits something either formally or by implication. By deciding what to accept and what to contest, it is the defence which creates the real dispute. For the reasons given, the main disputed fact will generally be whether the crime was committed, or whether the accused was the person responsible for committing it, but rarely both. The prosecution can usually prove the undisputed main fact without any difficulty.

At an early stage in the trial, which issue is in dispute will have emerged quite clearly.

As was seen, result-crimes – those which lead to tangible consequences – are less often in dispute because, as a rule, if they were committed, this is easily proved. Accordingly, in considering their finding, magistrates are unlikely to have much difficulty in holding that such offences occurred.

Where a crime involves some intangible element, such as a state of mind, or is itself an intangible type of crime, as in the case of a conduct-crime, a decision can be more difficult. Here, conflicts of eyewitness evidence are common.

In object-crimes, similar principles apply. Tangible facts such as the nature of an object will be easily proved, often by inspection of the article produced in court. Intangible facts such as the accused's possession of the article in a house are likely to be the issue.

Where the real dispute is about the identification of the accused, the ways of proving this must be distinguished. Visual identification at the time of the crime is only one type. Because of the risk of a miscarriage of justice through misidentification, recognition, which proves identity, should never be confused with resemblance, which is only an item of circumstantial evidence.

As was shown, each method of identification has its typical sources of mistake. In pre-trial procedures including descriptions, photographs, confrontations, Identikit, artists' drawings, or identification parades, a common risk is that identifications may be influenced unintentionally by discussion of evidence.

Circumstantial evidence of identity may vary from the suggestive to the compelling. Often real evidence by forensic scientists, for example fingerprint or DNA evidence, falls into the latter category.

In prosecution evidence of identity, the most common question is whether or not witnesses are mistaken.

Witnesses who are mistaken about identity may be quite sincere, and if so, their evidence may be very persuasive.

Lying about the accused's implication in the crime is also a fertile source of disputes.

In prosecution evidence, the main target of the defence may be that police witnesses are lying about confessions made to them by the accused. Even partial admissions falsely attributed to the accused could cure any defects in prosecution evidence. Such evidence requires careful attention.

In defence evidence about the accused's implication, lying is commonly suggested, about an alibi, for instance.

5. Direct or circumstantial evidence

If direct (eyewitness) evidence is accepted, it proves the facts to which it refers. Circumstantial evidence is more complex. It must be considered on three levels before it can prove any main fact which is in issue.

The first level is concerned with the relevant facts – those separate and secondary facts from which the main fact may be inferred, such as paint on a youth's clothing of the colour used by vandals on a wall. Often, proof of the relevant facts does not involve any great problem, especially where the witnesses are independent and unconnected with each other.

Drawing an inference from these relevant facts occurs at the second level of consideration. If the court infers the existence of one of the main facts in issue, that is, the commission of the crime or the accused's implication, it must be satisfied beyond reasonable doubt, for this to be valid. Care is necessary. Anything from a guess to an inevitable conclusion may be called an inference. Generally, the greater the number and variety of the relevant facts, the better the support for the inference.

In the above example of vandalism, if the youth was seen in the area when the wall was painted, an inference that he was the culprit would be stronger.

The third level of consideration arises when an incriminating inference from prosecution evidence clashes with a denial in direct defence evidence, which may destroy the inference pointing to guilt, or raise a reasonable doubt. In the example, the youth might claim that he got paint on his clothing when he found a can of paint and threw it away. Here, the direct defence evidence would have to be rejected before an inference of guilt could be made.

Apart from making inferences from proved facts to other facts, the essence of fact-finding is the detection of mistakes and lies.

6. Mistakes and lies

Inaccuracy in evidence arising from mistakes or lies was discussed previously, but some essential points may usefully be highlighted.

In forming a judgment, the distinction between mistakes and lies should not be blurred, although this occurs in poor advocacy, or occasionally, where the facts are obscure. The causes of mistaken and untruthful evidence are different. To confuse them means that attention will be directed to the wrong factors. If the witness does not or may not know the facts exactly, inaccuracy may be due to mistake. But if the witness must know the facts, inaccuracy must be intentional, that is, the result of lying. The witness's state of knowledge of the facts is therefore of primary importance, and this question should enter into the assessment.

An advocate's claim that evidence is mistaken may or

may not be persuasive, but is usually inconclusive if it is based on difficulties of observation or memory only. If the challenge has merit, it is more likely to relate to secondary facts or those which received insufficient attention. A report may be accurate despite hindrances arising in the nature of what is seen, the conditions of observation, the witness's state, the lapse of time, or the influence of discussion.

But even inconclusive challenges which fail to prove that important evidence is mistaken may still show that it is unreliable. In prosecution evidence, this could be fatal to conviction, as in the case of visual identification based on a fleeting glimpse in adverse conditions.

Two approaches may be taken to the assessment of honest evidence under attack as mistaken. One is that if a witness is trusted, his self-assessment of the accuracy of his evidence may overcome any criticisms of his observations or his memory. He was there; magistrates were not. If he is regarded as a sound and responsible person, and he insists on his evidence, this may carry weight.

But a contrary approach is that honest witnesses who testify with sincerity and are therefore convincing may still be mistaken, especially in visual identification evidence.

Which approach to take is a matter of judgment. No rules for fact-finding can be stated. While the material in this text is essential knowledge, nothing can replace the judgment of magistrates about how it should be applied in the particular circumstances.

Although mistakes in evidence are common, they usually concern secondary aspects of the main incident. But the crucial area of visual identification is known to be particularly vulnerable to mistake and the greatest care is necessary in judging such evidence.

Lying about essential facts is the biggest problem in judging testimony. Blatant lying occurs every day in criminal trials, despite anything which the law can do to prevent it. The previous warnings about the dangers of deciding credibility solely from an impression of the witness are again emphasized.

A witness's character, so far as it can be known in a trial, gives little guidance to the credibility of what he says, although it may create some distrust.

A witness's demeanour, by itself, is a shaky foundation for any important conclusions.

While lying is always to be explained by some motive, to grasp that a witness is motivated towards conviction or acquittal is inconclusive in isolation.

Impressions of character, demeanour and motive enter into judgment, but are too subjective to determine credibility safely, without other supporting evidence.

7. Belief and judgment

The ultimate nature of belief can be left to psychologists and philosophers. For the practical purposes of the magistrates' court, belief depends on three questions: (a) Do I trust this witness?; (b) Is this witness's evidence reasonable?; (c) How is this evidence related to other evidence?

A negative answer to either question (a) or question (b) would have the effect that the evidence would be disbelieved. It is not to be expected that a court will believe evidence given by a witness who is distrusted, or evidence which is unreasonable in itself. For belief, both of these questions must be answered affirmatively and then question (c) must be answered favourably.

(a) Trusting the witness

Warnings have been given about the risks of basing a view of evidence solely on a subjective impression of the witness. But to some extent, and inevitably, magistrates form impressions of witnesses in the course of every trial; it is natural for people to respond to each other intuitively. Thinking about the witness may also lead to a conclusion, such as "Has this headmaster come to court to commit perjury about a road traffic accident which he saw from the school window?"

A witness may be trusted in various ways – he may be accepted as truthful, or he may be accepted as reliable when he claims that his memory for an event is accurate.

The basis for proving facts in court is that decent citizens do their duty. The foundation of fact-finding is acceptance of an honest witness's assurance that he saw what he reports, although there is no absolute reason or compelling logical process which makes this belief inevitable. To accept any testimony is a judgment which includes trust. But justice depends equally on not accepting the testimony of mistaken or dishonest witnesses.

(b) Reasonableness of evidence

Here "reasonable" means that the evidence contains no major defects, in the sense of inconsistency or improbability. These have already been discussed. Either defect could be anything from a slight to an insuperable barrier to belief.

Trust in a witness is discussed separately from quality of evidence, but they are linked. If evidence is self-contradictory or absurd, a witness may not be trusted at all. Even where a witness is seen as both truthful and generally reliable, his evidence must still be reasonable for belief. Otherwise it may be regarded as mistaken.

Any believable evidence should stand up to objective scrutiny, that is, it should be reasonable in the sense defined above, irrespective of the witness who gives it. Overall this, rather than attacking the witness's credit, is the major approach to evidence in a trial. But it is in the course of an objective probing of evidence that the flaws in a witness, such as bias, dogmatism, and the turns and twists which indicate lying, emerge most clearly.

In reaching a finding, an objective analysis of evidence which exposes its defects is a sounder basis for rejecting it than an adverse view of the credit of any single witness. Unreasonable evidence is unlikely to be accepted as credible.

But the contrary does not hold. If evidence is reasonable, that is if there are no obvious defects in it, this removes an obstacle to belief, without necessarily meaning that this evidence is true, accurate and will be accepted. It simply means that it *could* be true and accurate; it can be described as plausible. Something more again is needed for belief – the relationship of the evidence in question to the other evidence in the trial.

(c) Inter-relationship of evidence

The superiority of a criminal trial over an enquiry made of a single witness in isolation rests on the possibility of comparing separate testimonies about the common facts. For belief, especially in finding guilt proved beyond reasonable doubt, evidence must be fitted into a context of other evidence.

As an illustration, a statement that England has been devastated by a sandstorm would be rejected because it is contradicted by facts which everybody knows.

But in a criminal trial the facts are fortuitous. For all that is known, they could be so or not. For evaluation, a context is needed into which individual items of evidence can be fitted for comparison.

By the stage of reaching a final decision, a context can be derived from the whole of the evidence led. Here, magistrates should compare everything in the trial, whether oral, documentary or real evidence, facts admitted, or facts conceded in speeches. What is in dispute will have been tested from various angles. Any single piece of testimony should be evaluated by reference to this mass of evidence, in which it can be said that the whole is more than the sum of its parts. This is what makes sound and confident decisions possible – not a hunch about whether or not an individual witness is telling the truth.

Items of evidence may be related by agreement or contradiction.

A body of evidence in which separate testimonies agree may have considerable weight, where conditions are favourable.

128

Where the witnesses are independent and unconnected with each other this may exclude the possibility of common error, due perhaps to discussion of evidence, or collusion to give false evidence. Their evidence may then be impressive.

But where these favourable conditions are absent, if the witnesses are motivated and associated with each other, agreement in their evidence may have a common source, by design or chance, and may be suspect − although it could, on the other hand, be accurate. Parrot-like similarity in the words used, order of topics, and odd features may create doubts.

Contradiction in evidence here refers to the normal conflict about facts between adversaries. It was distinguished from inconsistency, which exists in one party's version of the facts.

Contradiction is a key concept in evaluating evidence. It may complete the confrontation which occurs in destructive cross-examination. As was said, evidence challenged in cross-examination is rarely destroyed at that stage. But it may be so weakened that later it succumbs to contradictory evidence led by the cross-examiner.

It is constantly to be seen in court how this can be of great help in evaluating evidence. The evidence of any witness may seem to be perfectly plausible and to withstand cross-examination. Yet it must be rejected if magistrates believe a contradictory witness.

8. Reasons for finding

Magistrates need not, and usually do not, give reasons for their findings, but may do so. At times, to state reasons may be advisable; it may help in focusing the issues; it may be fair to parties and, indeed, if reasons are requested, compliance would be proper; it may avoid an appeal due to doubt about the grounds of the decision; if there is an appeal, the reasons will have been recorded at the time.